LUNATIC
WIND

LUNATIC WIND

Surviving the Storm of the Century

William Price Fox

Algonquin Books of
Chapel Hill
1992

For
Betty Gilbert
with love

Published by
Algonquin Books of Chapel Hill
Post Office Box 2225
Chapel Hill, North Carolina 27514-2225

a division of
Workman Publishing Company, Inc.
708 Broadway
New York, New York 10003

Excerpts from *Nets & Doors,* by Jack Leigh, used by
permission of Wyrick & Company, Publishers /
Ampthill Books / The Southern Images Partnership.
Excerpt from *The Killer Storms* by Gary Jennings.
Copyright © 1970 by Gary Jennings. Reprinted by
permission of HarperCollins Publishers.

Library of Congress Cataloging-in-
Publication Data:
Fox, William Price.
Lunatic Wind: Surviving the Storm of the
Century / by William Price Fox. — 1st ed.
p. cm.
ISBN 0-945575-42-4
1. Hurricane Hugo, 1989. I. Title.
F275.F68   1992
975.7'043—dc20   92-14303
CIP

10 9 8 7 6 5 4 3 2 1
First Edition

CONTENTS

Hugo: An Introduction and Confession   vii

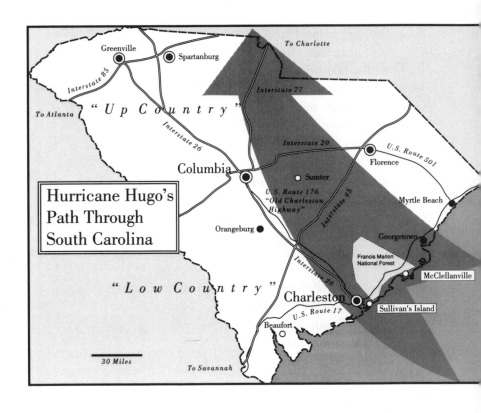

Hurricane Hugo's Path Through South Carolina

Greenville

Spartanburg

Interstate 85

To Charlotte

Interstate 77

To Atlanta

"*U p C o u n t r y*"

Interstate 26

Interstate 20

U.S. Route 501

Florence

Columbia

Sumter

U.S. Route 176
"Old Charleston Highway"

Interstate 95

Myrtle Beach

Orangeburg

Georgetown

Interstate 26

Francis Marion
National Forest

McClellanville

"*L o w C o u n t r y*"

Charleston

Sullivan's Island

U.S. Route 17

Beaufort

30 Miles

To Savannah

HUGO

An Introduction and Confession

To be honest, when Hurricane Hugo was 400 miles off the coast of South Carolina, the only thing that occurred to me was that it would bring some rain to Wildwood, where I play golf 100 miles inland in Columbia. I figured it would be great for the kids and their buddies to whip down to Surfside Beach—a favorite spot between Myrtle Beach and Georgetown—and get in some first-class surfing. In other words, like so many others in Columbia, South Carolina, I didn't think Hugo had an outside chance of hitting home. I also thought that Governor Carroll Campbell's evacuation order to clear the coast was the dumbest thing since the Republicans nominated Dan Quayle. The way I had it figured was the way almost everyone had it figured: the storm would veer north and hit Cape Hatteras or go on back out to sea where it belonged; Charleston and the "Low Country"—the low-lying rivers and swamps along the South Carolina and Georgia coast—would wind up with about a foot of rain; and the rainstorm would die down 50 miles from Charleston, right about at the Orangeburg exit on Interstate 26.

Anyhow, I actually played golf on Thursday, September 21, 1989, the day the storm would come ashore, and as I recall the morning sky was clear, the clouds were fluffy, and the wind was down. The course was browning out in spots, and in the grill room the conversation was golf and the fact that we needed rain. There are two television sets in the grill room. One was showing a baseball game, the other, Hugo's progress across the Caribbean. I'd take a blood-and-Bible oath that not

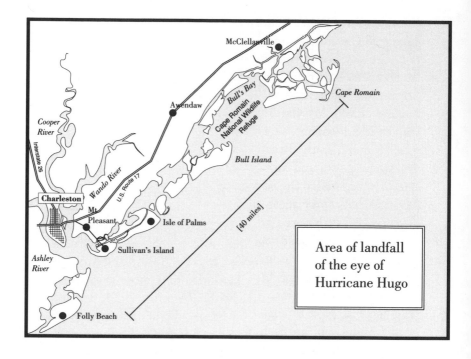

two of the men and women in the room were watching either one until some real estate type announced to no one in particular that he would lay fifty-to-one odds on the storm not hitting Charleston, and a hundred-to-one on Columbia. No one paid much attention to him. A few hours later I remember being sorry I hadn't gotten a couple hundred down.

That evening two families who live in Charleston on the coast came to my house in Columbia to wait out the storm. One family had been evacuated from their Sullivan's Island beach house so fast that they hadn't been able to find their big Labrador retriever and were more worried about him than their home. They, too, like almost everyone I knew, thought the storm would veer north and go out to sea, but when the evacuation orders had come from the governor's office they had to leave.

It was four in the morning and I was in bed when the 90-

mph winds at Hugo's front edge started chewing up Columbia. I went to the window and watched the trees awhile, wondered why the sky had turned a light green, heard the fire department sirens wailing down in Five Points, and went back to bed. There was no television or radio; the power had gone out around eleven. My visitors, who had a house outside Charleston, in Mt. Pleasant, as well as the beach house out on Sullivan's Island, both directly in the storm's path, had been phoning Atlanta and New York all night trying to find out how bad it was. Finally, the next morning, they were able to watch the first helicopter shots on a battery-powered television, as the news crews hovered over Sullivan's Island. While many of their neighbors' houses had been blown away, theirs had survived. Later that same day a National Guardsman heard their dog barking and found him in high spirits bouncing up and down on the front porch.

When I started to write this book I thought it would be a simple matter of gathering a series of survival stories and stringing them together into something whole. The idea was to take four representative families from across the state and sit down with them and let them tell how they coped with Hugo and how they recovered. I wanted to tell exactly what a storm of this size was like and find out how people are able to reach down inside themselves and find the strength they need to survive. And, finally, I wanted to tell what they had done with their lives after the storm.

The plan was simple enough: I'd write about the families before the storm, during it, and after it. Then I'd wrap it up with the aftermath, the rebuilding, and the political overtones, and probably end it with a quotation from Shakespeare or Lewis Grizzard and be back out on the golf course by May in time for the member-guest tournament. Well, now it's three years later. I found the four families and used up thirty or forty miles of audiotape, but nothing felt right. The families, despite their ordeals—some of which were incredible—had not really seen the storm much differently than I had standing at the window and watching the trees: they had seen only a small part of it. I interviewed more and more people, but kept running up against the same wall: no one, with the possible exception of Capt. Stan Salter, who rode his shrimp boat through the storm in the McClellanville Harbor with his lights on the village as it was literally picked up and destroyed before his very eyes, really saw Hurricane Hugo in all its massiveness and sweep. One obvious reason was that it struck around midnight and, like me, almost everybody was inside where they belonged.

So, I began reading. The material on hurricanes seems endless. Some of it, especially *The Killer Storms* by Gary Jennings, is wonderful, but except for an old Nordoff and Hall book called *Hurricane,* which later became a Dorothy Lamour and Jon Hall black-and-white movie, none of the books really let me see a storm or feel how it felt. So I turned to what I'm comfortable with, telling stories, to show what had occurred. In essence, the book you are reading is "docu-drama": I've stuck to the facts and the real events of what actually happened during that night and early morning, but have changed most of the names and created composite characters as a way of conveying what being in the storm was like.

Most of the material, except for scene-setting and actual dialogue, draws on the actual experiences of survivors. While some of the events may seem incredible, they are based on interviews or pieced together from similar occurrences that are documented fact. In what follows, I use fiction techniques for what I hope will convey the *feel* of the storm, and introduce those sections with brief nonfiction essays on the facts surrounding a hurricane so destructive it has been called "the storm of the century."

PART ONE

Thursday

1

Storm Warnings

During a hurricane men and animals do strange and unpredictable things. Dogs get quarrelsome. They yip and howl, whip around in little dog circles and can't stay still. On the other hand, cats seem to ignore the winds outside and often sleep right through the storm. Some fish will swallow stones so they can sink deeper and keep out of the way, while others are flung up on the shore where they quickly die. When fish built to withstand only deep-water pressure are brought to the surface by churning currents and waves, they explode. Shrimp and squid and sailor's choice simply go whichever way the currents and tides take them, whether to disaster on shore or to safety out at sea.

Birds, sensing an approaching storm and quickly discovering that the air is less buoyant, begin nervously flying lower and hopping along the ground. Once the hurricane arrives, many will drop down into the eye and fly along with it until the storm finally uncoils and collapses. But often the hurricane will last for days and the birds will find themselves hundreds and often thousands of miles from home. The cattle egret migrated to this country from Africa in a hurricane, and there are reports of refugee parrots from Mexico and rainbow-colored birds from the Yucatán jungles appearing in New York City and the snowy reaches of Canada after a hurricane has passed by.

The lower air pressure that comes with a storm allows gases and odors to escape from the soil where they are normally trapped. Horses and dogs, which are much more sensitive to smell than humans, react badly to this phenomenon and become high-strung and fidgety. And older animals, as well as older people suffering from rheumatism, will feel the pain as the low pressure causes the fluids in their joints to expand.

Only mankind attempts to control the power of a hurricane by denying it. No other creature will stand and watch a hurricane storm surge breaking over it, will try to race with its winds, ride a bicycle through its rain, or watch from an ocean view patio and raise a drink to it.

How members of other cultures have dealt with winds and storms in the past was described by Sir James Frazer in *The Golden Bough*:

> The Lenguas Indians of the Gran Chaco ascribe the rush of a whirlwind to the passage of a spirit and they fling sticks at it to frighten it away. When the wind blows down their huts, the Payaguas of South America snatch up firebrands and run against the wind, menacing it with blazing brands while others beat the air with their fists to frighten the storm. When the Guaycuras are threatened by a severe storm, the men go out armed, and the women and children scream their loudest to intimidate the demon. During a tempest the inhabitants of a Batak village in Sumatra have been seen to rush from their houses armed with sword and lance. The Rajah placed himself at their head, and with shouts and yells they hewed and hacked at the invisible form while an old woman was seen to be slashing the air right and left with a long sabre.

Herodotus tells how the ancient Greeks tried to stop the wind: "The storm lasted three days. At last, by offering victims to the winds, and charming them with the help of conjurors, the Magicians succeeded in allaying the storm." Then Herodotus adds: "Or perhaps it ceased of its own accord."

Until the invention of the telegraph in 1840, the only hurricane warnings came from ships, which would fly a storm flag for other ships nearby; there was no way of warning the people on the shore. This, then, would partially account for the terrible death toll of 300,000 in 1737 in the Bay of Bengal when a cyclone came ashore. But before we draw too many smug conclusions about improved communications technology from this, the same type of cyclone struck Bangladesh in 1991, leaving 150,000 dead. So while the Bangladeshis were warned of the impending disaster, the country was too disorganized and too poor to evacuate the cities on the coast and move the people back to higher ground.

We are more fortunate in this country. Today, with radar, television, satellite photography, and the presence of "Hurricane Hunter" planes, which fly into the very eye and keep us informed of the storm's every move, there is very little reason why anyone should be killed in a hurricane if calls for evacuation are heeded. But even with this knowledge, and the electronic sophistication we have today, facing a major hurricane is still something that only the naïve take lightly. No one who has ever gone through one forgets it.

By the first week of September of 1989, the dog days in South Carolina were over and school was back in session. The weather was clear and getting cooler, and up near the mountains around Greenville and Spartanburg people were already wearing their corduroys. At the Texaco station, a gallon of unleaded at the self-serve pump was $1.04, and with the elections more than a year away, the only posters on the telephone poles were about Jesus.

Other than local shootings, a few drug busts, and high speed chases, South Carolina stayed out of the news. But a week later, on September 13, off the west coast of Africa, something big was brewing. Certain wind, moisture, and heat conditions were coming together and staying together long enough to form something called Tropical Depression Number Eleven. A day later, Tropical Depression Number Eleven strengthened into a Tropical Storm and was given a name. It was called Hugo, which means heart and mind: a strange name with an Edgar Allan Poe sound about it; it was ominous. It would get stronger and more ominous as the next seven days went by.

————

It was 2 P.M. on September 21 and Roscoe and Jay Derrick, Billy Simms, and Mike Watts were counting their money in the Winn-Dixie parking lot across the street from Dreher High School in Columbia, South Carolina. It came to $63.20, and they began laughing and jumping around and slapping each other on the back. A half hour later they'd lashed their surfboards to the top of Roscoe's battered Volvo station wagon, bought three family packs of Kentucky Fried chicken, and were all set for their drive to the beach, a hundred miles away. Hurricane Hugo was four hundred miles from the coast and the word was out that the waves were five and six feet high.

Roscoe was crowing, "Man, those waves. Those waves are going to be awesome. We can get there in two hours and surf till dark."

Mike, the oldest, kept repeating, "Beer! Beer! We need beer."

Jay slowed the car to stop at the light in Five Points. "We need a damn adult. Okay, Roscoe, any bright ideas?"

Roscoe began machine-gunning his hands on the dashboard to the music of a B-52s tape. "Turn right and keep going. We've got to have it. Hurricane waves. Man."

They cruised by two Minute Savers, but both places Roscoe said, "No, not here. Keep driving." Near Elmwood he saw the cashier he was looking for. "Check it out. He's got to be from Taiwan or Korea. Hell, maybe he's Chinese."

Jay looked over. "What if he calls the cops?"

"Don't be stupid. Check him out." Roscoe raised the corners of his eyes with his thumbs. "They all look alike to us and we all look alike to them. Hell, he can't tell if we're sixteen or sixty."

Billy Simms climbed out, lighting a cigarette. "I'm coming with you." His red hair almost matched the rose on his Guns 'n' Roses T-shirt.

Roscoe tucked his shirttail in. "Okay, man." He licked his fingers and smoothed his hair down in the side mirror. "Put your shoes on. Maybe you ought to get some Cokes so we don't look suspicious."

Roscoe waited until the cashier was busy with Billy and the Cokes, and then he slid a twelve-pack of Busch onto the counter along with five jumbo packs of pork skins. The man didn't say a word while he was counting out the change.

Then he spoke. "Would you like something else?"

Roscoe was dying to get out of the place. "No thanks."

The man seemed grateful and smiled. "Have a nice day."

Back out in the car, Mike and Billy were screaming and pounding Roscoe on the back as Jay waited until a slow-moving dog was out of the way. He was furious; they'd just drawn straws over who was going to drive—and not drink—and he had lost.

Mike said, "Man, that was so cool." Every time Mike said "cool" he raked his blond bangs down over his eyes.

Billy turned around laughing. "You looked great in there. I swear, I'd have sold you beer."

Roscoe popped open a can and, ducking down below the window level, he took a long drink. He sat up, wiping the foam from his mouth. "Man, that dude was so stupid. You should have seen that grin on him."

Billy said, "Yeah, he looked just like Jay."

Jay slammed his hands on the steering wheel. "Shut up, man."

He was almost out of the parking lot when Roscoe grabbed his shoulder. "Stop the car. This is just too good to waste." He went back in the Minute Saver and came back out grinning with another case on his shoulder. "Listen, y'all, this is one spot we keep quiet. Okay, dudes?"

Mike, in the back seat with his feet out the window, said, "Damn right."

Billy and Jay agreed, too, and they pulled out and headed back across town. Coming into the interchange out by Heathwood Hall School, they saw the problem. And just as they saw it, they heard it on the radio. Governor Campbell had called for an evacuation of the Low Country and southbound Interstate 26 was closed to everything but police and emergency equipment heading for Charleston. Jay stopped and, making a U-turn, he headed back across town toward West Columbia and U.S. 176, the Old Charleston Road.

By the time they had passed Dixiana, ten miles southeast of Columbia, one sixteen-piece box of chicken and half a case of beer were gone. Jay kept telling everyone to slump down in the seat and keep the cans out of sight. Mike whispered to Roscoe about spending the whole night at Cindy Murdock's house when her parents were out of town.

Jay checked him in the mirror, laughing. "That's not the way I heard it."

Mike mimicked his high voice. "Okay, wise guy. Exactly how did *you* hear it?"

Jay kept grinning in the mirror. "Janet said Cindy told her you were too scared to even kiss her."

Mike kicked the back of his seat.

Jay shouted, "Hey! Cut the crap! You want us in a damn wreck?"

Roscoe had his shoes off and one leg slung out the window. He was on his fourth beer. Suddenly he shouted, "Stop! Goddammit!"

Jay pulled over. Roscoe jumped out and, leaning on the door, he began throwing up. Mike, Billy, and Jay were howling.

Billy said, "Aw, man."

Roscoe was still hunched over in the weeds. "Just shut the hell up, will you?"

Mike laughed. "You got it all over your stupid shoes. Jay, give big brother your shirt."

Jay laughed and turned the music up.

Two minutes later Roscoe was his old self, drinking a Coke and chewing on a chicken leg. "Man, I hear hurricane waves run ten to fifteen feet, sometimes twenty. This is going to be so cool."

A few miles north of Goose Creek they still hadn't seen a single police car or any sign saying they couldn't go on to the beach. But 98.7 FM WAVE, out of Charleston, was telling them an entirely different story. All of the barrier islands, including Seabrook, Kiawah, Sullivan's Island, and the Isle of Palms, had been evacuated, and no one was allowed to go there unless it was an emergency.

Jay kept worrying about it. "How're we going to get out there?"

"We'll think of something," Roscoe said. "Just hang tight."

At Goose Creek they pulled up to a phone booth at a service station and Roscoe called a friend in Charleston, who said that no one could get out on Sullivan's Island because the bridge had been closed off to all traffic except residents who were leaving.

Jay was drumming his fingers on the steering wheel. "Let's forget it. We can pick up Seventeen and go to Garden City or Surfside. It's great surf there and we can park right down by the water."

But Roscoe knew the beach and the waves out at Sullivan's Island and, in case they wanted to spend the night and surf all day the next day, he knew they could go to the house of their Dad's friends Don and Tracy Rideout. Sullivan's Island was definitely the place to go.

Finally Billy called one of his cousins, who told him they could use his rowboat to cross the channel. The boat was tied up at the pier near the last bridge and the key to the lock was taped under the seat. It was perfect. They would row over, beach the boat, go surfing, drink the beer and eat the chicken, and then come back. Or maybe they'd stay all weekend.

Roscoe said he'd seen the shots of the surfers riding the waves off of Oahu. "But nothing is going to touch this. You got any idea how big they get in a storm like this?"

Jay looked over. "How big?"

"Fifteen, twenty feet easy. Sometimes bigger, man, and get this, there's no waiting. I mean capital N capital O, NO WAITING."

Out at the pier the boat was there and the key was there and after loading up, they were on their way to ride the big waves. As they rowed across the narrow channel, the wind was howling and the water was chopping and the little boat had to be crabbed far to starboard to keep on course. Roscoe and Mike paddled hard to keep it from getting broadsided and capsizing. Slowly they made their way to the point. And then they saw the ocean.

Roscoe pumped his fist in the air. "Man, look at that! Look at that! This is so cool! No one gets waves like this."

Mike gave him a high five. "And no one's going to be out there but us. Look at it. Jesus!"

The waves were as big as the ones Jay and Roscoe had ridden out in California. They were rising up and cresting out as far as they could see. Roscoe was right, there would be no waiting for the perfect one. These were *all* perfect. They were over six feet high, with spray blowing off the tops, and they kept coming and kept coming. There would definitely be no waiting.

2

Old Friends

As you approach Columbia from the north, the red clay rises slightly and begins to flatten out. The road widens and gets smoother and there may be crape myrtle and wildflowers planted in the median; even the drainage ditches are landscaped. The Chamber of Commerce and the Highway Department are preparing you for your first glimpse of the capital. And then you see it, the brand new skyline with the old green dome of the capitol building in the center. It's the same dome that Sherman aimed for from his position across the Congaree River in 1864. The city is on a plateau that was once a plantation owned by one Mr. J. T. Taylor, who went public with the outcry, "They ruined a damn fine plantation and built a sorry-assed town."

But there it is under the reflecting clouds, illuminated like something out of a fairy tale or Disney World or the Land of Oz. The gold and silver buildings and the green dome of the old capitol are too flashy and too bright to be called sophisticated or tasteful, but there it is: Columbia.

A string of bronze stars set into the western side of the capitol marks the places Sherman's shells hit home. They have been there since the Civil War and they will probably be there forever. And at the front of the capitol is a statue of George Washington with his cane broken off. Underneath is the explanation that when Columbia was occupied, the Northern soldiers "brickbatted" it. That too will remain there, along with the statues of Robert E. Lee, Wade Hampton, and the Hon.

James F. Byrnes, who is gazing reflectively out over the azaleas at the corner of Sumter and Gervais.

After the road widens and you get close to town, you run through three or four miles of franchise food signs and cartoon-colored neon. You could be anywhere in America. You could be in Fort Worth or St. Louis or Anaheim, but after a while you'd know that there was a difference. A big difference. For this is a town that Sherman burned to the ground, and while most of the natives have forgotten that fact, many have not. There is still a big mural in the downtown Macy's department store showing Columbia in flames. And above the back bar mirror at the Capitol Restaurant there are two old photographs of Main Street. One shows that boulevard before Sherman came through town; the other, after he had it burned. History, then, has shaped this city as it has few others. In the oldest section, the streets are named for the Revolutionary War generals: Sumter, Marion, and Bull. In the newer sections, they bear the names of Confederate leaders: Lee, Jackson, Bratton, Pickett, and Greene. One of the biggest and longest-running controversies in the city is whether to fly the Confederate flag from the statehouse. As of this writing, it is still flying beneath the Stars and Stripes and the indigo blue state flag. But the winds of change and modernization may soon bring it down.

The old capital city is a study in contrasts. Out on the fringe you can still find general stores that sell night crawlers, blood-worms, and crickets to fishermen, and dispense candy from a curved glass case to kids. You'll see smoked hams and mule collars along with fan belts hanging from the ceiling, and out front between the gas pumps will be a slick wooden bench where the old timers play checkers and watch the traffic going by. Against this rustic reminder of the forties and fifties the city claims three ballet companies, fifteen-story buildings of steel and glass, gourmet restaurants, and nonstop air service to New York City, one stop to Los Angeles.

Columbia is the home of the University of South Carolina, USC, which has grown from an enrollment of 4,000 students in the fifties to a present-day enrollment of 30,000 at the campus in the heart of town. There is a medical school, a law school, and for the last two years the USC School of International Business has been rated among the nation's best by *U.S. News & World Report*. The city also prides itself on having eight legitimate theaters, beautiful inner-city parks that sweep down along the Congaree River, and a very successful Philharmonic orchestra. The most recent addition to the USC campus and the city has been the Koger Center, a remarkable 4,000-seat auditorium with one of the best sound stages in the country.

Mainline tracks from the old Atlantic Coast Line, Seaboard Air Line, and the Southern Railway all run through the town, and at night you can hear the boxcars from today's CSX and Norfolk Southern trains rattling along them, and the lonesome cry of their big diesel engines. Some things in Columbia have not changed and probably never will. Kids still lay pennies on the tracks, bet nickels on who can walk a hot summer rail the longest, and still press their ears to the tracks listening for the trains. Small boys still tie their sweaters around their waists and little girls still travel in squealing threes and fours, hugging their books. And there will always be a kid and a dog and a scene on the way to school. "Go on now, Queenie! Go on home now." But Queenie will have other plans, and she'll lay her ears flat and slide along the drainage ditch like she's invisible until finally the kid gives in. "Doggone it, Queenie! Now, don't you be out here at recess. You hear that?"

Columbia is like this—small, quaint, and country—yet there is a remarkable sophistication and liberalism you might not find in many much larger and better-known metropolitan areas. The university attracts a large Asian student body, and the U.S. Army's Fort Jackson has an even more cosmopolitan makeup. Twenty years ago the only foreign food you could get in Columbia was pizza. Now there's everything from Vietnamese to Turkish to Indian to take-out sushi. The schools have been integrated since the sixties and are working as smoothly as those anywhere else in the United States, and better than most. And today, at a time when whites-only country clubs are under attack all across the nation, five of Columbia's six clubs are integrated.

For a long time Hollywood portrayed South Carolinians as bowlegged, overall-wearing hicks who ran funny down dirt roads, slapping their thighs and shouting, "Eeeee Haaaaa." But most of this image has now faded. Indeed, probably one-third of the residents of Columbia are from other parts of the country. Many Fort Jackson soldiers originally from "up North" decided that they were tired of fighting the snow and traffic and high taxes back home, and when they mustered out or retired, came back to settle permanently in Columbia.

The Congaree River runs right through the center of town and not only can you canoe through downtown Columbia, you can catch record-breaking striped bass right inside the city limits.

Roscoe and Jay's father, J.C. Derrick, always thought he had a sense of humor and he could take anything. But what had happened playing golf out at Wildwood had been too much. He had hooked into the woods on four holes, caught the water on the eighteenth, and his usual 80 to 82 had shot up to a humiliating 96. He'd lost $28 and had to pay for the sandwiches and the drinks. But worst of all, his partner, in a booming master-of-ceremonies delivery, announced the 96 to everyone in the bar and presented him with the booby prize that now sat beside him. It was a small bronze statue of a tormented golfer watching a miserable shot. At the golfer's feet were the withering words, "Better luck next time, only not here please."

Heading home at three o'clock, J.C. was still furious as he turned his air conditioner on super cool. The sky was clear and the wind was down as he pulled out of Alpine Road and onto Interstate 20. At the bar there had been talk of a hurricane heading for Charleston. It was the same hurricane that had been heading there for three days now, but the oddsmakers were saying that it would veer north toward Cape Hatteras and go back to sea where it belonged. Already it had hit St. Croix and Guadeloupe. But for J. C. Derrick, who was still thinking of his miserable tee shot on eighteen and his miserable score and who didn't even know the name of the hurricane, it was like an air crash in Bolivia. It didn't matter.

In front of him a Trailways bus began flashing its braking lights and slowing down. The Interstate heading west and back into Columbia was jammed, and he cursed and took his Buick out of automatic cruise and slowed. He was on a high curve and behind him he could see a long line of traffic; it was barely moving. Many cars had their lights on; some had even stopped. It looked like a South Carolina–Clemson football caravan. But the license plates were from Ohio, North Carolina, and Tennessee, and the back windows were so loaded down with luggage and beach equipment that the drivers could barely see what was behind them. J.C. slumped forward with his chin on the wheel. "Now, just what in the flying hell's going on out here?"

The bus stopped and J.C. stopped behind it. Clicking the radio through a sermon, a country-and-western tear-jerker, and a series of commercials, he finally found the news on 560 AM. Andy Thomas was announcing that Hurricane Hugo was still heading northwest, and Governor Carroll Campbell was thinking about evacuating the entire coast. Then J.C. figured it out. The cars were filled with tourists from Myrtle Beach; the hurricane reports had scared them and they were heading home.

J.C. was stuck behind the bus all the way onto the Bull Street extension and into Columbia. As he pulled into his driveway, he saw a big black custom-made Lincoln parked in front. Even if J.C. hadn't seen the license plate, MAX #1, he'd have known who it belonged to.

Max Rosenthal was on the front porch holding an old-fashioned, wooden handled shopping bag while J.C.'s dogs barked and lunged against the door. J.C. opened the door, and holding the sheepdog, Phoebe, by the collar, he let Max in.

Dooley, the golden retriever who would bark but wouldn't bite (and who Fanny, the cleaning lady, said would hold a flashlight for a burglar), picked up a ball and began circling Max with it, nudging him to throw it for him. Phoebe was another matter. The hair on her neck was straight up, and J.C. had to stick his knee in her side to keep her from biting him. Not until Max had put his hands in his pockets and was standing still did she finally stop growling and settle down.

Max had just driven in from Myrtle Beach and said the whole beach was pulling out and heading inland, and he wanted to spend the night. He had brought along three bottles of sangria, six limes, a pound of cheese, and a half-gallon of Smirnoff 90-proof vodka. They would watch football on television and plug J.C.'s boys into a few movies on the VCR upstairs. Max, like J.C., was divorced. But he had been living alone for three years; this was J.C.'s first year. His ex-wife was in California with her new husband; he had stayed in Columbia with his two teenaged sons, his dogs, and his job in advertising.

J.C. was examining the picture of a dancing *señorita* on the label of the sangria—it had been bottled in Chile and looked suspicious to him—when the phone rang. He let it keep ringing until the answering machine cut in. It was Elise, his younger sister, and he let the machine take the message. The tape was old, so there was static, but he could hear her loud and clear. She was in town and had just driven up from Charleston.

"J.C., this is terrible. Momma wouldn't come with me and I'm worried sick. That hurricane is heading straight for the Battery. Anyhow, I'm coming right over and I'll fill you in on everything. Oh, and I want to stay with you tonight." Her voice was soft and syrupy, pure Charleston, but it was also insistent.

J.C. shrugged his shoulders at Max. "Sorry, old man."

Max smiled thinly. "That's a tough break. When that gal looks at me I feel like something that has to be flushed a couple of times."

She and Max had not gotten along since Max made a pass at her at the South Carolina–Clemson tailgate party three years back.

J.C. and Max took their drinks into the living room and turned the television on. WIS-TV was posting a weather update, saying that Governor Campbell had just issued the official evacuation order for the whole South Carolina coast—from Hilton Head Island to North Myrtle Beach—everyone was boarding up and getting ready.

J.C. sipped his drink. "God, can these people be serious? Can you imagine a hurricane hitting Charleston?"

"You know what the big joke here is?" Max asked. "It's the first time the weatherman gets a story and the anchorman takes over."

J.C. rattled the ice in his glass. "And don't you know that the politicians are eating this up. Hell, all they'll have to do is say what they did during Hugo and that's their campaign."

Max raised his glass. "I'll drink to that."

The phone rang again. It was the cleaning lady, Fanny, and she wanted a favor. She usually asked for money and she always got what she asked for. It was a game they'd been playing for six years now. But this time it wasn't money. She was frantic. Her younger sister was in Columbia visiting their mother, who was in the hospital, and she'd heard the news that the little coastal town of Mc-Clellanville, where she taught school, was being evacuated.

Fanny said, "Mr. J.C., that hurricane's scared all these brothers of mine and their children up from Charleston and I just don't have any more beds. Could she stay in one of your rooms? I'll be glad to bring some food to tide you over."

"Fanny, you just bring her on over. The more the merrier. And I don't need a thing. Thanks anyway."

Fanny was laughing. "Mr. J.C., the last time I looked in that icebox of yours, there wasn't nothing in there but Coca-Colas and an old bag of carrots. I'm right here at the Piggly Wiggly."

"No, Fanny, I've got everything covered. Just bring her on over. Does she smoke?"

"Yessir. She smokes Kools. But she's got her own."

"Fine, that's fine. All I've got are a few cigars. Oh, by the way, where the hell's McClellanville?"

Fanny laughed. "Honey, it's out in the woods up the road from Charleston. But don't ask me how to get there."

As J.C. hung up, the front doorbell rang. The dogs started barking again and J.C. locked them up in the kitchen. It was Don and Tracy Rideout. J.C. hadn't seen Tracy in months but it was hard to forget someone like her. Almost impossible. It wasn't really so much her looks as the way she used them, a trick known to only a handful of women. "Look what the hurricane blew in," she purred, kissing him on the cheek and hugging him. "We tried to phone you, but it's a madhouse out there."

Don and Tracy had known Max for years. She hugged him and Don shook his hand and slapped his back. As the men carried her matching tapestry luggage in from the porch, Tracy took her jacket off, dropped it over a chair, and flipped her long black hair off her shoulders. "You ought to see the lines out there. Telephones, bathrooms, gas stations. People are lining up for everything. Lord, it took us forever to get here."

Don held his hands out and pretended they were shaking. "Look, twenty miles an hour for five hours. How's that for a day in the country? Boy, if you don't have something to drink, I'm going to short out."

Max rubbed his hands together like a miser. "I brought some sangria over, the original stuff. Tell you what I'll do. I'll make you both one. You're going to love it."

Tracy smiled at him. "What's that Number One for on your license plate?"

Don answered for him: "Divorces. No one can touch him."

Max grinned and, pointing a pistol finger at Tracy, fired off a round. "Y'all read what Grizzard said about divorces? Said the next time he's going to save himself a lot of money and grief by just finding himself a woman he hates and then giving her a house."

Max served the sangria over ice and raised a toast. "To old friends."

Don said, "Yeah, it's been a while." He took a long drink, frowned at the taste and then forced a grin. "Great stuff." Then he changed the subject. "I bet we saw fifty cars overheating."

"Fifty!" Tracy snorted, stirring her drink with her finger. She didn't like it either. "There were fifty in that last rest stop. Lord, we saw people *walking* out there. Everybody's petrified of this thing."

Suddenly her voice dropped and her mood changed. J.C.'s sheepdog, Phoebe, had just strolled into the room and, recognizing Don and Tracy, sat down and waited to be noticed. Tracy got down and hugged her. "Don, you swear Buckles is going to be all right?"

He patted her shoulder. "I swear to it, baby. He'll crawl right up under the house and be as snug as a bug. Now you've just got to quit worrying so much." He tipped his drink at J.C. "Is it okay if we stay the night? This thing ought to blow over by morning."

J.C. nodded at Tracy's bags. "You can stay, but that luggage has got to go."

Tracy stood up, brushing Phoebe's hair off her black leather skirt, and smiled at J.C. "Come here, you. I need another hug."

"Jeopardy!" was on the television but all of a sudden the beeping of a weather flash got everyone's attention. They all moved into the living room. The local station had cut in and was showing a color blowup of the satellite picture of Hugo. J.C. adjusted the color on his brand new thirty-six-inch Sony and got the orange out of the red and the yellow out of the blue. The huge cloud system looked like it would easily cover North Carolina, South Carolina, and Georgia. The shot also showed how fast it was moving and where it was going. To J.C., the swirling concentric circles, one red, one yellow, and one blue, looked like something alive and crawling one moment, and one of Van Gogh's whirling nightmare moons the next. But then he just shrugged it off. It had been the same old

story every year since he could remember: the storm would head
for the beach for a couple of days, get strong enough to rattle the
palmettos and drive the tourists back to Ohio, then it would move
back out toward Cape Hatteras.

"Jeopardy!" came back on, and J.C. switched channels to another
station that had another satellite picture on the screen. The weather
man had outdone himself tonight and had on a tie with a quail in
full flight over a crouching bird dog. He was monitoring and map-
ping the progress of Hugo and announcing that the storm had now
been upgraded to a Category Four Hurricane, nearly as bad as a
hurricane could get, with winds of up to 155 mph. It was traveling
due northwest at 20 mph and heading right for Charleston.

The picture changed to an overview of the houses along Rainbow
Row, moved on to the City Market, then swung around and came
down King Street. The camera was shaking in the wind and paper
and leaves kept blowing by. Don and Tracy crowded in close when
the camera panned across the storefronts. They were hoping that if
they looked hard enough they could see their advertising office behind the Mills House Hotel.

Don whistled and pointed at the huge satellite picture that was
now filling the screen. "Man, this is getting serious. What do you
think, J.C.? Is it going to hit?"

Max had taught physics in high school before he went into public relations. He touched a spot on the TV map and started explain-
ing what they were seeing on the screen. "They usually get right
about in here and then they hook on up north. We'll just give it a
little more time. It should turn pretty soon."

Tracy said, "Well, it damn well *better* start doing something. It's
running out of room and my dog is still out there."

Don wrapped his arm around her. "There, there, baby. It's going
to be all right. J.C., you don't think it's going to hit, do you?" he
asked again, ignoring Max and hoping J.C. could get Tracy's mind
off her dog.

But Max kept rolling on. "Category Four is right up there with
Camille. No, Camille was a Five. Hell, they had a 200-mile-per-

hour wind and it killed three or four hundred people." He sipped his drink and hooked his head approvingly. "But you know something, if this thing decides to hit Charleston, this could be much, much worse."

Tracy buried her face in her hands. "Don!"

Don glared at Max. "Boy, you're a big help."

But now Max couldn't be stopped. "And, you know, Camille hit small towns. I'd say we're looking at maybe two hundred thousand people down on the coast. Hell, maybe more. Max pointed at the upper right edge of the red circle. "Now here's what you've got to watch. Right in here is where it's the strongest and does the most damage. If it moves north just a little, it'll miss Charleston and hit my house in Myrtle Beach."

Don squeezed Tracy's arm. "See there, baby. Myrtle Beach, not Sullivan's Island."

Max was still oblivious. "Hell, I wouldn't mind it hitting me. I could use a new roof and a paint job. Maybe even a little landscaping."

All the local bulletins were off for the time being, so J.C. switched to CNN, where Storm Davis was busy bringing the whole country up to date on Hugo. He turned the sound up. "Well, this is sure as hell putting the old Palmetto State on the map."

3

A State of Mind

South Carolina is relatively small. You could put it in the top right-hand corner of Texas and it wouldn't reach downtown Dallas. Year in and year out the old Palmetto State leads the nation in poverty and infant mortality and hovers near Mississippi and Arkansas down at the bottom on SAT scores. It's also right up there near the top of the charts in teenage pregnancies and aggravated crimes, and when it comes to death by snakebite in religious services, it's the undisputed champion. In fact, it's the only state in the union where snake handling is legal in a house of worship. There is also a law still on the books that says a woman can be put in jail on the grounds of being a common scold. In 1790 the penalty was public dunking, but in the next century it was changed to three days in jail. With all this going against it, why doesn't everyone just simply pack up and head north or west? Many do. But eventually most of them come back.

People keep coming back and tourists keep settling down because the weather is mild and, despite a few drawbacks, it is one of the better places in the country to raise kids. There's Little League baseball in every town; there are swimming holes and fishing holes; deer, dove, and duck to shoot; and over 200 miles of beaches that the state tourist office touts as some of the best in the world. The cities aren't too big, and even in the biggest of them you'll see an occasional possum crossing the road at night. In the small towns three and four dogs at a time will lie safely out in the middle of the intersection, and town drunks still sit and sleep under the chinaberry trees.

The newspapers still have the good sense to report a suicide as "after a short illness" and in many places a parking ticket sets you back just a dollar.

Another reason people don't leave is simply the great good humor that seems to attend every event from the Chitlin Strut to the Okra Strut to the Catfish Stomp and the Gizzard March. The curious come from all over the "hard lard belt," which stretches out to western Mississippi, to see what they're all about. There are state fairs, county fairs, town fairs, and fairs jerry-built at crossroads, with sawhorse tables for the pies and the pickle relishes, and rides that fold down from the back of pickup trucks. Sightings of "The Lizard Man," "The White Shark," and "Swamp Thing" make the legitimate papers every three or four months and are regularly bannered across the local tabloids. And only a death, a divorce, or an armed robbery with aggravated assault will free up a ticket to the South Carolina-Clemson game or The Masters right across the border in Augusta, Georgia.

The outrageousness of politics and politicians in the Palmetto State have matched, and probably beaten, anything dished up by the Lone Star State or Louisiana. One old pol in the 1940s, running on what he called the Truth Platform, announced, "I can envision the day when only the living can vote." Alexander Sanders, who recently left his job as Chief Judge for the Appellate Court of South Carolina to take over the presidency of the College of Charleston, is famous for saving a big stand of cypress trees from being cut down by announcing that he had personally sighted the ivory-billed woodpecker. In a television show about South Carolina, he was filmed sitting in his judicial robes twenty feet up in a deer blind in a tree in the swamp, reading a law book.

Sanders is also credited with the prescription for the perfect season for the South Carolina Gamecocks football season. "Five wins and five losses. That way the University is happy, the coach gets to keep his job, and the athletic department won't mutiny and take over the school."

Establishments such as the Capitol Restaurant in Columbia, 82 Queen in Charleston, and The Old Pro's Table in Myrtle Beach are renowned for their politicians, their sages, and their metaphysicians. Max Gergel, who invented the now-defunct insecticide "Sam Chewning's Roaches' Last Supper" (which featured a drawing of twelve roaches sitting at the da Vinci table), dines at the Capitol. On the night before the Chitlin Strut, when asked who would eat a chitlin, he held forth as follows: "You take a man and tie him to a post for three days and three nights and feed him nothing but bread and water. On the fourth day he will eat a fried chitlin. He will not like it, but he will eat it." Then he spread his arms in the image of crucifixion. "Grease, that's the secret of South Carolina. It's what keeps us all together. Hell, you go into a store and ask for something like safflower oil and they'll think you're a member of the Red Menace."

In Charleston, John Kruse, a businessman who will occasionally take a glass of sherry at 82 Queen before dinner, said that the secret in South Carolina's success was something a little more romantic than grease. "It's barbecue. South Carolina barbecue will cross that finish line as tender as pound cake and, with our sauces and light bread and coleslaw and cold beer, it will drop you to your knees, where you will weep tears of appreciation and never-ending gratitude. I personally have seen serious men in business suits and full grown Christian women go into what is called a 'barbecue coma.'"

And out on the sands of Myrtle Beach, at the Old Pro's Table, where the talk is golf and only golf, the consensus is that South Carolina's main attraction is, and will continue to be, the sun and rapid-growing Bermuda fairway grass. "It's a bonafide fact," one gentleman with a low handicap is credited with observing. "There's 80 percent less insanity down here than up in New York and New Jersey. And the reason is we get sunshine every day. Once you get above North Carolina, you get cloud cover four and five months a year. And when a man can't see his shadow for that long, his timing gear starts slipping. If he doesn't get some fast front-end work, he's in real trouble."

Humor, grease, barbecue, and the sun are tangibles, and may be what keep the natives tending to their collard patches and hanging gourds for the purple martins. But there is something else much harder to put your finger on. It's something that makes the old drunks want to die here and makes the unwed mothers drag themselves onto Greyhounds and come back here to have their babies.

Whatever it is, it seems to make the natives believe that nothing is going to happen too fast, that one day is almost certain to be like the day before, and the day before that. There is no danger of the mercury plunging to minus 30 degrees and staying there, or of a four-foot snowfall paralyzing the cities, or of a plague of locusts darkening the sky. The sun shines almost every day, the winters are mild and usually quite pleasant, and you can escape the summer heat by going to the beach or the mountains or by waiting until the sun sets and sitting out on the porch. It is out of this that a certain sense of well-being and comfort emerges. Everything seems so predictable, so unchanging. It is no wonder, then, that most South and North Carolinians' reaction to Hugo's approach was the same as for any hurricane—the storm would turn north, and while there would be some wind and some rain, nothing serious would happen. They had no doubt that by September 22, the day after the storm, the corn, the tobacco, and the soybeans would once again bathe in the sun's golden light, and the football and political season would be in full swing.

Jay and Roscoe had been riding surfboards since they were in
elementary school, but last summer was their first time on the big
waves. They had spent their vacation with their mother and her
new husband and had ridden the surf out at Zuma Beach, north of
Los Angeles. They had loved it, and Beth-Ellen had bought them
expensive, double-finned Hobie boards with yellow decks and red
bottoms and enough surfing outfits to last through college. The
only problem was that once they'd surfed there, South Carolina was
boring by comparison. But today, with Hugo pushing the waves in
high and fast, they knew they were going to get all the big ones
they could handle.

It was after four, and Hugo was still reportedly six to seven
hours away, when they stashed the beer and the chicken under a
lifeguard barrel and swam out about a hundred yards. They climbed
on their boards to wait for the right wave, but Roscoe was right,
there was no wait. The waves were rolling in steadily, five, six, and
seven feet high, and the wind was blowing the spray fifteen and
twenty feet in the air. They were perfect waves and, looking behind
them to the east, for as far as they could see, there was no end to
them.

Jay was still a little scared, but he was determined not to show it.
"Roscoe," he said, "this is bigger than Zuma."

And Roscoe, who was standing up on his board, crouching over
an air guitar, shouted, "Awesome! Awesome! Totally awesome!"

They surfed for two hours straight, then they took a break.

Roscoe shielded a chicken leg under his arm to keep the blowing
sand off. "I wish we'd brought a camera. No one's going to believe
this."

Jay was laughing. He wasn't scared anymore. "This is the greatest. They're twice as big as Zuma."

Roscoe popped open a beer. "And ten times more of them." He
took a long swallow and wiped his mouth. "Hell, make that a hundred."

They had already surfed two hours more and it was getting dark when Jay and Billy saw the blue lights flashing and the policeman standing on the car roof shouting to them over a bullhorn to get out of the water. They paddled in and dragged the boards onto the beach. At first they didn't see the television van that was panning them for the Charleston news. When they did, Jay waved at the cameraman but Billy ducked his head and kept looking at his feet.

The policeman raised his voice over the wind. "Well, if this isn't the limit."

Jay, trying to sound as innocent as possible, said, "Yessir? Anything wrong, sir?"

The policeman was mad. "You know you're the only people on this whole damn island? Just how did you get out here, anyway?"

The wind was howling and the sand was flying. He leaned over so Jay could hear him. "Any more out there?"

Roscoe and Mike were lying down flat behind the waves and if he told on them he knew he'd never hear the end of it.

He shook his head. "No sir, just us two."

Billy said, "That's right, sir."

The officer kept looking but he didn't see anything. "Come on, then. Let's get out of here."

He put them in the backseat and turned the engine on. Then, taking one last look up and down the deserted beach, he climbed in and headed back for the Ben Sawyer Bridge and the mainland.

He checked them in the rearview mirror. "Y'all aren't from around here, are you?"

Billy said, "No, sir. Columbia."

"That figures. Did y'all know anything about the evacuation?" But before either of them could say, "No, sir," again, the policeman raised his hand in benediction. "Forget I even asked that one."

Roscoe and Mike watched as the patrol car with the surfboards sticking out the windows drove away. They were hiding in a trough between the waves and lying as flat as they could get. When the car vanished, they rode a quick series in and sat down at the lifeguard's barrel.

Mike was scraping the sand off a chicken breast with a plastic fork and looking for a place to bite. "They aren't going to tell on us, are they?"

Roscoe popped open a beer. "Hell, no. Jay knows I'd wipe him out if he did. Hey, the wind's picking up."

The sand was blowing harder and he could barely make out the road behind them. He drank his beer and watched the wind whipping the sea foam up over the sand dunes. Suddenly the waves seemed even higher and they were coming in so fast they were running together. He dropped his empty can. "Let's hit it!"

Mike hesitated. "Man, it's getting rough out there. Are you sure?"

"Damn right. We've got to shoot one or two, so we can say we did it."

They raced in but the wind and surf had become stronger, much stronger. Keeping the noses of their boards low and paddling as hard as they could, they only got out about fifty yards. They were fewer than ten feet from each other, but they had to yell to be heard over the wind. Roscoe glanced around and suddenly it scared him. He'd never seen waves so big, whitecaps so high, and spray so thick that he couldn't see—not even in the movies. The waves were so close he couldn't tell where one ended and the next one began. He wanted to shout, "Awesome!" but all he could do was choke down his fear and nervously begin turning his board for the shore. Mike did the same.

Suddenly, out of nowhere, a monster wave peeled up and caught them by surprise. They were being lifted up fast, too fast; it was as though they were on a roller coaster. They were holding onto their boards, pointing straight up, and there was nothing underneath but air. Behind them was another big one, and behind that, another. They seemed to be coming from all directions. They were flying toward the shore. When the first wave dropped them, another picked them up, and pushed them higher. Then it happened—Roscoe's board was ripped from his hands, then Mike's. They were falling. Both knew how to tuck and roll when they hit but now, with their arms and legs flailing, they were out of control.

A wave slammed them into the sand. A second held them there

and ground them in. Roscoe landed on his shoulder and, rolling over and over, he finally skidded through the small stones and shells to a stop. He got up dazed and gasping and crawled for the beach.

Mike hit so hard on his back he blacked out for two or three seconds, but he managed to get to his feet. When he staggered in, he was almost in shock. They both were skinned and bruised and out of breath. Roscoe didn't say a word. Mike couldn't.

The foam, mixed with sand and salt, was whipping up in long shreds, wrapping around their arms and legs, stinging their skin and burning their eyes. They slicked the slime off with their fingers, but as fast as they did, the screaming wind brought it back, this time mixed with long strands of seaweed and kelp. Tearing it off and too scared to even look for their boards, they started running for the closest house. As they ran, a sudden gust picked the lifeguard's barrel up ten or fifteen feet in the air, dropped it carelessly, and sent it hurtling end over end down the beach. The chicken went with it, and almost immediately the sand covered up the rest of the beer.

Roscoe and Mike were huddling under one of the oceanfront beach houses. They were cold and they were frightened. They didn't know what they were going to do next. Most of the house owners hid their keys near the door, usually on top of a beam or under a flower pot, or hung them on a hook under the siding. But they had looked in every conceivable place and found nothing. Roscoe wanted to break a window but Mike said no. They were already in enough trouble dodging the police without adding breaking and entering.

Roscoe's teeth were chattering. He knew they were about 400 yards from the end of the beach and that if they kept going to the right, they would eventually come across Don and Tracy's house. It was named "Dun Roamin" and was pink with purple trim. He'd been there two or three times before and he thought he knew where they left the key. "Mike!" He had to scream to be heard. "Come on!"

"Where we going?"

"Just come on!"

The sand was blowing so hard it was stinging their backs and legs and faces. They had to cover their eyes and look straight down. Something sharp hit Roscoe's shoulder, and when he touched the spot, it was bleeding.

"Damn!" He had to scream in Mike's ear. "It's clam shells!"

"Yeah, me too. Man, they're killing me."

Roscoe kept going in the direction of Don and Tracy's, but the blowing sand was so thick he couldn't see more than five yards ahead. Beneath him he saw another sign of the wind's power. The sea oats were being pulled up by the roots, and clam and oyster shells were sliding along the sand as if they were being pulled by a magnet. Hunched over and trying to look forward, he and Mike made their way up the beach for another hundred yards. Then he saw the pink house and they headed for it.

Underneath Don and Tracy's house they searched for the key. The wind was higher and Roscoe shouted, "It's near the door. I've seen him put it there a million times."

Something moved in a dark corner under the house and it scared him. It was Buckles, Don and Tracy's yellow Labrador. "Hey, Buckles." Roscoe patted his knees. "Come here, boy." The big dog wagged his tail and rubbed up against him as he petted his head. "Boy, how'd you get out here?"

Mike shouted, "Man, there ain't no key here. Come on. Let's break a window or something."

Roscoe kicked a pane of glass out of the back door and reached in and flipped the lock. His shoulder was hurting from the fall he had taken and still bleeding from the clam shells.

Once inside, Mike headed for the telephone, Roscoe for the television. Roscoe automatically picked up the remote and turned the TV on, then he called over, "Who you calling?"

"My folks. They're going to be worried sick."

Roscoe grimaced. "Just hold up on that. When this thing blows over, we're going to look like idiots. It should be on the news pretty soon."

"Blows over? Are you crazy? It's getting worse." Mike was looking out the big front window and couldn't believe his eyes. The waves were up even higher, and as far out as he could see, it was nothing but raging ocean and towering whitecaps. "Damn, man, look at it."

Roscoe, ignoring the view and "The Andy Griffith Show," was wrestling with Buckles. "Come on, man, get with it, these things never last." He rolled over and, with a headlock on the big dog, he gazed out the window. "Boy, we've got the best seats in the house. Look at it. Oh, man, what I wouldn't give to be out on those babies right now."

Mike pretended to stick his finger down his throat. "Oh, throw up. Man, you are such a fake."

Roscoe opened two cans of Heineken, handed one to Mike, and with two bags of potato chips they sat on the floor and tried to find an MTV show. "Man, this is so cool. Look, he must have a hundred damn movies. I wonder if he's got any porno? This is going to be wild. Hell, we can even build a fire."

Mike finally relaxed and stretched out on his back, examining the bigfish net studded with seashells and starfish that decorated the ceiling above them. "You know something, this is my first Heineken. Damn, this stuff's good. Too bad it's so expensive." He sipped his beer and began counting the starfish in the fishnet. "Roscoe, you know what I wish I had right now?" He smiled. "Cindy Murdock, that's what."

"Man, now that would be true heaven," Roscoe said. He had crawled across the floor and was looking through the videos. "Shit. There's no porno here. Just a bunch of exercise tapes."

"Yeah. Cindy."

Roscoe grinned. "Maybe she could bring Marjorie along."

"Yeah."

Roscoe got up to feed Buckles. There wasn't any dog food, but there were six eggs, so he broke them into a big bowl and filled it up with crackers and bread. Then he laid five slices of raw bacon across the top. The dog wolfed down the bacon first. As he was working his way through the rest of the meal, Roscoe and Mike watched television.

Mayor Joseph Riley was talking from City Hall in downtown Charleston. His voice was controlled and firm, but his thin hair was blowing in every direction. "The citizenry must not be lulled into a false sense of security. Hugo is a dangerous, killer hurricane, and the combination of winds and high tides could produce a storm the likes of which few people in Charleston have ever seen."

Roscoe said, "Look at that, will you. All that skinny bastard is trying to do is get him some votes. Everybody knows it's going to turn."

But Mike glanced nervously out the window and stared at the beach. It was dark but he could still see the bright whitecaps and the streaming foam. "But let's just say it doesn't. Turn, I mean. Roscoe, can this place hold together if that thing hits us?"

"It's not going to hit, stupid."

The dog had finished his food and was looking around for something else. Roscoe rubbed his head and gave him the last of the bacon and a quarter pound block of butter. "Besides, even if it did, you think Don Rideout's going to build something that's not going to stand up to a little wind? Man, he's cool."

"Yeah, yeah. Hey! Jesus, check this. Look what the damn water's doing." The rain was sweeping in horizontally now, and the water was running *up* the window instead of down.

"Creepy," Roscoe said.

Tiny shells and small pebbles were clacking like typewriter keys on the big picture window and next door, in the shaft of light from the porch, a Century 21 sign was spinning around and around.

But Roscoe was firm. "I don't care how strong it is. I'm saying this house can take anything that *any* storm can dish out."

They watched the waves as the television announcers reported that the power companies would soon be cutting the power off at the main sources to prevent fires and gas explosions. Roscoe quickly checked the phone, then he started looking through the cabinets for a flashlight. "Hey, Mike. Let's give Cindy a call. How about it?"

"Yeah, man." He jumped up and began dialing. "Maybe Marjorie's with her."

Roscoe found a two-cell Eveready flashlight in the closet. He slid the switch and it worked. "Any luck?"

"Nah, man, it's busy. I'll bet it's busy all day."

"Yeah, she's probably yakking to that fat what's-her-name, Julie."

And then, just as Mike hung up for the fifth time, the lights flickered and the room was suddenly dark. "Whoaaa dudes! They weren't kidding," he said. Roscoe turned the flashlight on and, after skimming the beam around the room, he aimed it out at the ocean, which was now rolling in over the dunes. The wind had picked up and, as they watched the Century 21 sign turning faster and faster, they felt the house beginning to tremble.

Mike looked over. "Maybe we ought to be calling our folks."

Roscoe frowned, "Yeah, you might be right. But let's give it a little more time. This stuff can't last."

4

Low Country and Up Country

One of South Carolina's dubious claims to fame is that there are said to be more poisonous snakes there than in any state in the nation. Seven varieties can be found in the Low Country woods and swamps. Beaufort County, known locally as the rattlesnake capital of the world, provides most of the rattlers for national carnivals and sideshows, for antidote serum, and for religious services. Along with the rattlesnakes you'll find the cottonmouth water moccasin, the copperhead, and the deadly coral snake. During and after Hurricane Hugo, the prevalence of these snakes was to be one of the greatest worries. The snakes left the swamps, swam to higher ground, and climbed into the trees to wait until the waters receded. People reported seeing as many as twenty in one tree. While there were no reported deaths by snakebite, the threat of it lurked in the branches of every fallen limb and every standing tree weeks after the storm had passed.

Framed by magnolias and sweet gums, and absorbing the tannic acid coloring from the cypress roots, the rivers of the Low Country take on the color of old whiskey. Alligators and great blue herons thrive along the banks. There are still bear in the woods, and lynx, fox, red wolves, and wild turkey. The Kiawah Indians, who not only encouraged the English to settle there, but gave them considerable help during the first years, are long since gone.

Back during the Puritan reign in England there were statutes on the books against "vagrants, rogues, vagabonds, stage players, and sturdy beggars." This same intolerance found its way into the Americas where the Puritans, the Quakers, and the Pilgrims who settled there had no use for theater, or the arts, or almost anything connected with leisure. Low Country South Carolina was not settled by these grim sects, however, and it became a haven for traveling actors. As early as 1703 there were staged shows. Charles II and his friends loved the arts, the artists, and the theater. It's appropriate that South Carolina, named for him, would follow suit. More theaters were built in Charleston in the early eighteenth century than anywhere in America. King Charles also loved horse racing, music, dancing, formal gardens, raising dogs—even golf. All of these, plus an abundance of good whiskey, came to early Charles Town. When the Puritan Yankee Josiah Quincey visited the city, he concluded: "Cards, dice, the bottle and horses engross prodigious portions of time and attention; the gentlemen—planters and merchants—are mostly men of the turf and gamesters."

While Restoration England cast the psychological mold that Charleston and the Low Country were to follow, it was the West Indies island of Barbados, with its huge exportation of slaves to the region, that shaped its economy and much of its architecture. In 1674 there were 50,000 whites and 80,000 blacks living on that island. Some historians suggest that Charleston and the Low Country existed solely to take in the overflow of slaves from crowded Barbados. In any event, the heritage is undeniable. In eighteenth-century Barbados, long before Charleston was laid out, there was a Bay Street, a Broad Street, and a St. Michael's Church; features carrying the same names would form the center of historic Charleston. Some of Charleston's famous architecture had its origins in Barbados, and the colony's first slave code—and the form of slavery itself—were copied from the Barbadians.

Unlike many of the strict settlements of the north, "the city by the sea" bred religious tolerance. As early as 1697, Huguenots, Jews, and Quakers lived side by side, preoccupied with the same problems: finding enough space to build on upon the tiny peninsula and keeping cool in the summertime. They built "single houses" modeled on those in Barbados—one room wide and with two rooms on each floor, set perpendicular to the street. Long piazzas built on the south and the west sides of these houses made them cool in the summer evenings and warm on sunny winter mornings.

By the mid-eighteenth century, the same principles that produced the Cavalier-Roundhead antagonism in England were at work in South Carolina, in the rivalry between the Low Country and the Up Country. A classic Low Country man, regardless of his wealth or his poverty, can still recall his glorious ancestry and the noble stock from which he sprang. One of the oldest jokes on the boards runs: How are Charlestonians like the Chinese? And the answer: They eat their rice and worship their ancestors. The Low Country man fishes and hunts, and he takes great pains to entertain his friends with the ease and graceful hospitality for which Charleston and the surrounding countryside are still famous.

In almost complete contrast to the Low Country man, the Up Country man, living only 140 miles to the north and west, might as well be from Nova Scotia. His ancestors, probably Scotch-Irish and German, were of a more fundamental, stern stock than their coastal cousins. The Up Country man, though, is not without his own cherished history. He fought at Cowpens and King's Mountain, and was there when the British were broken and driven out of the state. And he was also there during the Indian wars. John C. Calhoun, the great apologist for states' rights and slavery—as well as temperance—was born in Abbeville and is probably the most famous representative of Up Country South Carolina.

Unlike the Low Country man, the Up Country man was not at all averse to appearing interested in the making of money—in whatever manner possible. His forebears had worked hard in Europe running small farms. When they came here, they did the same, scratching a living out of the red clay and sand. They worked their cotton, corn, and sweet potato farms for generations, but in the end the land gave out and the price of cotton dropped. Leaving the farms, they moved into the textile mill towns and have been there ever since.

In 1800 the jealousy between these two parts of South Carolina became so intense there was fear of an uprising. Up Country men, who were increasing in numbers, demanded political rights which, up until then, had been given only to Low Country men. Finally, to solve the problem, the capital was moved from Charleston to Columbia, chosen because it was in the dead center of the state. With this move, political power gradually shifted to Columbia, where it has remained to this day.

Despite the differences between the Up Country and the Low Country—which have modified and smoothed out over the last hundred years—South Carolinians are proud of their history and proud of their state. They are also the only Southerners who have no secret envy of Virginia.

Back Up Country, where J.C. and his friends sat glued to the television, CNN was showing footage of the destruction at Guadeloupe and St. Croix. The Red Cross had responded quickly, and soup and medical lines had already formed on the tiny islands. The tin roofs of the houses had been stripped away, and square yards of Sheetrock and whole shells of shacks were strewn across the landscape, piled so high it looked like a windstorm had whipped up a landfill. Huge billboards were bent and twisted over and touching the ground, and telephone and electric poles had been snapped in half like pencils. High voltage lines could be seen flashing, and one shot showed a black-and-white dog barking at a popping wire until someone pulled the animal away.

People were walking around downtown St. Croix dazed, not

knowing what to do or where to go; some were looting shops right in front of the camera. Kids and grown-ups were throwing bricks and garbage cans through the storefront windows. Other places, people casually strolled along, pushing shopping carts from store to store, and gathering goods as if they were ready to get in a check-out line. Many would stop and chat, and some would even stop, strike a showman's pose, and hold up a new television set or a pair of Adidas shoes so the camera crew could get a good picture.

The police seemed to be just standing around. Looters were crisscrossing the street, almost as if they were playing dodgeball; the background was in chaos; the high voltage lines were sparking: the world down there was coming apart.

J.C. said, "Well, dammit, that's one thing that won't happen in Charleston."

Don agreed. "Not if Reuben Greenberg has anything to do with it."

"Who?" J.C. said.

Don frowned. "Damn, J.C., he's the chief of police. You ought to know that."

J.C. lied. "Oh yeah, I just forgot his name."

Tracy, who had calmed down some, asked Max what he thought about the looting.

He reached over and put his hand on her knee. "You can't stop looting, sugar. I was in Puerto Rico when Agnes came through and you should have seen it. Everybody was doing it. I mean kids five and six years old. Everybody is related to everybody, so what are the guards supposed to do, shoot their uncles and grandmothers?"

She picked Max's hand up and placed it back on his lap. "Lord, that's awful."

The news cut from St. Croix to a helicopter shot twenty miles south of Columbia on Interstate 26. The cars were bumper-to-bumper as far as the camera could scan; they had come to a complete stop. CNN anchorwoman Lynn Russell took over, announcing that southbound lanes to Charleston were closed. At the rest area near Orangeburg, overheated cars were parked with their hoods raised, steam and smoke rising, and people were carrying water to cool them off in everything from kids' beach pails and plastic bags to drinking cups.

One camera panned out over the National Welding Company and an area in the middle of I-26 where J.C. remembered four years back five people had died when the low rolling chemical smoke from the factory had clouded the highway long enough for a string of cars and trucks to crash together and burn. Today, nothing about that accident was even mentioned.

The weather map again showed the whirling mass moving closer to the shore. But now it was showing signs of wavering, and Lynn Russell said it was definitely giving every indication of veering north. She quickly added that any veering would be good because the eye, at that very moment, was still heading straight for the Battery in downtown Charleston.

J.C. heard a car honk outside and knew it was Elise. He got up, looked out the door, saw her park, and watched as she came up the walk smoothing down her beautifully tailored bone linen suit, which matched her expensive bone-colored shoes. As he opened the door for Elise, Fanny drove up with her sister, Olly May Thompson.

After the introductions, Fanny called J.C. back to the kitchen.

"Mr. J.C., I told you you didn't have no food here. What you going to feed these people with? All you got is coffee and some old dried-up bagels. Why don't you give me some money and let me go get something?"

"No, Fanny, you got kids to take care of. Now, come on, you get out of here. We'll be fine."

He walked her to the front door and watched her climb into her car. Then he couldn't help but stand there for a few minutes more and look up at the sky. It was a clear blue, the kind of blue it seemed you only saw in Columbia, with just a few soft, white clouds floating around; hardly hurricane weather.

Max, who had been switching the remote control from station to

station, had finally found something. He called for everyone to
hurry back to the living room. J.C. ran back in.

"Check this out," Max said.

WIS Weatherman Joe Pinner was on the Columbia airwaves
warning everyone that any town in the predicted path, which was
now from Charleston to Myrtle Beach and right across the state,
was in grave danger. All mobile homes should be evacuated. He
smiled his winning smile and warned his viewers to stock up on
water, batteries, candles, matches, kerosene for lamps, and any
foods that required no refrigeration. He reported that all schools
had been closed, all churches closed, all meetings canceled. When
the cameras tracked down Ocean Boulevard and the King's Highway in Myrtle Beach, the wind was howling and the clouds were
down on the deck. The plywood over the shop windows and the
doors and the crisscrossed masking tape over the bare plate glass
gave the town the same look that J.C. had seen on Guadeloupe.

Boat owners on the coast, Joe Pinner said, had already been informed that it was too late to do anything but tie their equipment
down and get inland. The main thing for everyone to do was to get
in their cars and drive as far inland as possible, as fast as possible.
Once again he announced that Interstate 26 and Interstate 20 were
closed to all shorebound traffic, and that anyone with an overheated car was instructed to pull well over onto the shoulder and
park until it cooled down or catch a ride with someone else. Then
he smiled at the anchorwoman, Susan Aude Fisher, and asked her
to take over.

Olly May Thompson was sitting on the couch watching the
screen, saying nothing. It would be dark soon, and she was worried
about her husband, Horace, and their twins, Wanda and Tonya.

Max patted her hand, even though he didn't know what was
wrong. "It's okay, dear. It's going to be all right."

"No. No, it isn't." A tear was trailing down her cheek. "I never
should have left. But how was I supposed to know?"

Max, not one to lose a chance at comforting a pretty woman,

tried to get her mind off her worries. "Did I hear Fanny say you taught school?"

"That's right," she said, taking out a handkerchief. "I teach fourth. Sometimes I teach the fifth. Oh, those poor little children. They're going to be so scared." She had a rich Gullah accent and Max had to listen close to follow the fast patter and the way she ran her words together. She sighed again. "I feel just terrible. But I just had to see my momma."

Max asked, "How's she doing?" He wasn't even sure what was wrong with her. He hoped it wasn't something embarrassing to talk about.

"She's just fine. She loves to go to the hospital." A trace of a smile touched her lips. "She's got what she calls 'the big knee.' It's a side effect of her diabetes."

Max said, "I never heard of that one. Here, let me make you a drink."

"No thanks, I don't drink."

He poured her a glass of sangria over ice anyway. "There's not enough alcohol in this to wet a stamp. Come on now, just sip it."

She watched the screen in a daze, not believing anything she was hearing.

J.C. sat down on her other side. "Fanny didn't tell us anything about you, except you were her younger sister. And that you were pretty."

Olly May clicked her fingernails on her drink.

Max smiled his brightest smile. "But Fanny didn't say *how* pretty."

This finally loosened her up some. "You boys are too much," she said. Then she started back on her husband, Horace. "Now what in the world is he going to do with his boat? Oh, he loves that boat so. Didn't they say all boat owners should leave them and head inland?" Her voice had a quick rhythm that seemed to rise above and fall below the words. "Didn't they just say that? About leaving?"

"That's what I thought I heard," J.C. said.

Olly May told them that her husband owned and operated a shrimp boat out of the McClellanville dock. He'd named it "Olly

May" and he just finished paying for it. She stared into her drink. "I know that man and he wouldn't leave that boat for all the money in the world."

Max put his arm around her. "Honey, tell you what we'll do. Let's go call everyone that's got a phone down there and find out what's going on. How about that?" He got up and offered his hand to help her up off the couch.

Olly May followed him, still talking as if Max hadn't said a thing. "I hope he'll take it back up one of the creeks. He's invested every penny we've got in it. But Lord, then he's got to deal with the kids. Oh, I don't know. I don't even know where they are, or who's taking care of them."

Max led her to the study phone. "Here, you come on with me. We'll find out what's going on."

He sat her down at J.C.'s desk. "If we have to make a hundred calls, we'll make them. We'll keep calling until we find everyone. And don't you go worrying about the bill. This is on old yours truly."

5 〜

McClellanville

These are the words of Archibald Rutledge, South Carolina's first poet laureate, in 1937:

> When you pass out of the peach and tobacco country of North Carolina and come to the moss-hung live oaks, the towering yellow pines, the supine Negroes, the dreamy waters of the coastal country between Wilmington and Charleston, the strange spell of that lonely land begins to take hold of you—if anything can. And when you drive slowly over the great three-mile bridge spanning the mighty delta of the Santee, a bridge over a shimmering wilderness of greenery starred with aquatic wildflowers, you come to . . .

. . . McClellanville. Rutledge was born in McClellanville on October 23, 1883. He attended the high school there, and the Porter Academy in Charleston, graduated from Union College in Schenectady, New York, in 1904, and taught English for thirty-three years at Mercersburg Academy in Pennsylvania. He retired in 1937 to devote his efforts to full-time writing and to the restoration of his plantation home, The Hamptons, back in McClellanville.

In his book, *The Woods and the Wild Things I Remember,* Rutledge gives the following account of a boyhood spent on the river and in the village:

> Every day the rice-planters drove from "The Village" to their places along the river, returning about sundown. This performance had the regularity of a ritual. I occasionally

spent a day with my father at our plantation home [The
Hamptons], but in the summer I preferred the coast, the salt
marshes and the sea breeze. During my boyhood years in
McClellanville, I was not idle. I became a commercial fisher-
man, working alone. I learned the haunting names of the famous spots of the vast sea marsh, names such as Eagle
Hummock, Oyster Bay, Five Fathoms Creek. On good days I
might catch one hundred good fish that I could sell. I had my
regular customers and sold a "string" of twelve fish for
twenty-five cents. I fished both by day and by night and loved
the exhilaration and the adventure of it all. I remember how
I loved to sell fish to an old gentleman who weighed about
three hundred pounds. He always bought a string for the
family and one for himself.

David Doar, in his 1890 sketchbook, lists only six houses in
McClellanville in 1860; in his *Rice and Rice Planting* he notes
that isolation was a physical fact that haunted the leading cit-
izens of the town almost from the beginning. Though only
forty miles north of Charleston, the village remained remote
to an astonishing degree:

In the beginning the trip in could take a week. Needless to
say, efforts to connect the town to the outside world were numerous and continual. . . . Despite the efforts of a well-
intentioned citizenry, the villagers had, at least for a time,
remained cut off—they pressed their noses against the well-
worn window of the candy store and looked on helplessly as
the world passed them by. In the long run it was for the best,
for while the benefits of progress had often eluded them, so
had the pitfalls, and what remains, even today, is a relative
charm and quiet. . . . Poverty is another matter. . . . [T]he
surrounding community never recovered from the Civil War,
and with a few years excepted, the main business of agricul-
ture was declining during this period. Still, no one was
starving. . . . The members of extended families, the kind

that have all but disappeared today, looked out for each other
. . . and together they brought living proof to John Ruskin's
dictum, "There is no Wealth, but Life."

In the long run, being cut off from the rest of the world forced
the people of the village to rely on intelligence and ingenuity.
H. T. Morrison, another resident, recalls,

"Here in McClellanville was built the first rice pounding mill
of the world, one of the first sawmills run by wind, the first
gasoline motorboat to carry freight and passengers in the
state, the first artesian well put down between Mt. Pleasant
and Georgetown, and the first mail carried by automobile in
the South.

The term "the creek" was used to cover that expanse of
marsh and waterways between the mainland and the Cape
Islands of Cape Romain, and a person who made his living
there was a "creek man." Fish, oysters, shrimp, and crabs had
always been caught in abundance and were a mainstay of the
village diet, but owing to the isolation and the lack of refrigeration, there was no market for them beyond the immediate
area until after World War II. Despite the isolation and the
lack of material wealth, from all indications, McClellanville
seems to have been one of the most delightful places in
Charleston County to grow up in. Typical of the pleasant life
there is this single day, described in the "McClellanville Social
News," *Charleston News and Courier,* on August 27, 1929:

Special: Mr. and Mrs. L. A. Beckman gave one of their en-
joyable all-day picnics at Cape Romain Thursday for a large
number of their friends. These occasions are annual affairs
that are always looked forward to.

Two boats, "Happy Days" and "Carolina," took the crowd,
numbering about 110, to Cape Romain Island 7 miles from
McClellanville. While most of the party bathed in the surf on
the front beach, some of the men drew the seine at the Cove,

where a large number of fish were caught. A fire was built of logs on the beach and the fish were cooked and served hot, with hot rice and coffee. Oysters were brought on the beach and roasted. A regular picnic dinner was spread under a large canvas canopy, including a barrel of grape juice lemonade, and all did full justice to the feast. On the return trip, all joined in singing songs of the old favorites, as well as the new popular songs, and reached home about sunset.

H. T. Morrison, in a 1960 letter to columnist Ashley Cooper, of the *News and Courier,* also tells about the early days when the village was almost completely cut off from the world. The residents' main concern was how, and how fast, they could get to Charleston, Morrison says. Since a large part of the inland waterway route was by way of shallow and narrow creeks that went dry at low tide, larger boats traveled by ocean. Smaller boats, having to stick to the inside waterways, often took a week to make the trip.

The shrimp boat captains of today work long, hard, painful hours. Since there is no guarantee they will find shrimp, and there's always the constant danger of foul weather and the loss of everything they own, the vocation attracts a proud and independent type of person—a maverick in today's world. But while shrimping is lonely and dangerous work, it is touched with a rare and ritualistic beauty that keeps the captains and the strikers coming back. Jack Leigh, in the text that accompanies his photographs in *Nets & Doors,* beautifully captures the daily rhythm of the shrimpers' life:

I began each day well before dawn, meeting the captain at the shrimp docks. The strikers were already on board, carefully pulling through the nets, searching for any tears and mending them with net needles and twine. Chains, ropes and winches were checked and prepared for the day's work.

The quietness of the surrounding marsh was abruptly shattered as the shrimp boat's engines were started. We made our way through the dark waterway to the open sea; diesel fumes and the pungent smells of salt and strong coffee filled the air.

As the captain neared his chosen fishing grounds, the outriggers were let down, spreading out from the boat like giant metal wings. A fusing and creaking winch was brought to life as the waterlogged, wooden trawl doors were set out. The bag at the end of the net was tied shut to capture the elusive shrimp.

The sea around us rolled black and eerie as the nets were thrown over the sides. Work lights from nearby shrimp boats provided a welcome camaraderie during that lonely and murky time before sunrise.

At dawn, the nets were lowered to the bottom, the drag nearly bringing the boat to a halt. A thick whiff of frying bacon cut through the early morning chill as the strikers cooked up a hearty breakfast. The captain flipped on the radio and called across to other boats pulling their nets in the dim light. The conversations were always the same—Where are the shrimp?

Anticipation swelled as the huge nets were finally pulled from the sea and the contents spilled on deck. The sight was startling, as a profusion of shrimp and unknown sea creatures slithered, wiggled, and flopped around. The strikers quickly pulled up small wooden stools to this writhing mound and with seasoned hands began culling and heading the shrimp, returning everything else to the sea. Sea gulls swarmed, screeching and feasting. The shrimp were sorted by size and iced down in large storage bins beneath the deck.

Throughout the day the nets were dropped and hauled in several times. As evening approached, the nets were hauled in one last time, the captain and crew hoping for that one big catch.

Trailed by the ever present flock of sea gulls, we "headed for the hill." The outriggers were folded up once more, show-

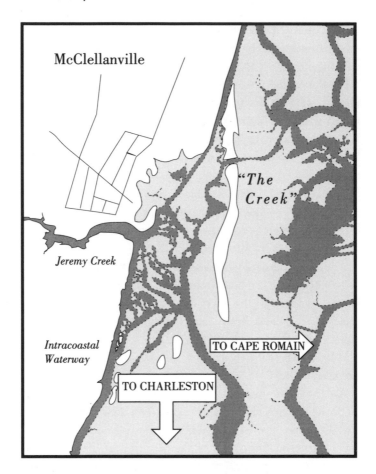

ing stark against the pale sky of nightfall. Sea-heavy nets were hoisted above the deck, shaken free of any accumulated debris, and hung to dry. The deck was hosed down and the boat was made ready for the next day when the sea and the shrimp would beckon once again.

This, then, is how shrimping has been done since the thirties and how it was still being done on September 20, the day before Hurricane Hugo struck. Many of the shrimp boat owners, hearing the warnings, took their boats and crews down the coast to Savannah, and even as far south as Jacksonville, Florida. But most of the captains who were still operating out of McClellanville thought the storm would curl north and head for Cape Hatteras; and if it didn't swing north, they felt safe remaining in the McClellanville Harbor, as it was considered one of the safest harbors on the coast.

―――

In McClellanville, Olly May's husband, Horace Thompson, had taken the twins, Tonya and Wanda, to the designated evacuation site at Lincoln High School. After that, and with every piece of rope he could find, he'd tied his sixty-foot shrimper to the pilings in front of the fish house. Hugo was still hours away and when he was finished anchoring the boat and storing his nets, he knew he had plenty of time to batten down his house. There was an old adage that went, "When the wind holds the plywood against the window, then you start nailing it on."

Horace licked his forefinger and stuck it in the air. A soft breeze had come up over the oaks and he could see the clouds barely beginning to move.

With a can of Miller High Life in one hand and a Black & Decker steel tape measure in the other, he took his time circling the house, measuring the windows for plywood. It was a six-room clapboard he had built himself, with wooden shingles and a breezeway down the middle. Four windows at the front were the same size, four-by-seven, but the rest were all different, and he had to be careful as he marked down what he would need. If the storm did hit, he wanted the plywood to cover the windows tight.

Horace had plenty of half-inch plywood and plenty of three-inch double-headed roofing nails that would be easy to pull out once the storm had passed. After sliding sixteen sheets out from the garage and into his pickup, and loading up two sawhorses, he drove around to the front yard where he could cut the stack of boards down to size with his chainsaw.

The plywood was cut and Horace carried it out and leaned it against the side of the house. He'd already crisscrossed and sealed most of the windows with heavy duty Mylar tape, but putting up the boards alone was going to be hard. He wedged his steel ladder up against the house, held the big sheet up over the jamb, and drove a nail in the center of the bottom edge. Climbing the ladder, he rotated the sheet up and anchored it at the top. After securing the top corners, he stepped down a few rungs and spotted the nails along the long sides, and at a few places where the sheet bowed out, leaving a gap. Then he moved on to the next window.

Once Horace started working, he worked fast. He'd set the nail with one tap, drive it in with three more, and then move on to the next one. His radio hung by its strap from the ladder pad and he kept the volume on high, listening to reports on the hurricane. Then it came, the news he was hoping for. It wasn't official, but the announcer was now saying that the storm was wavering and looking as if it were heading for Cape Hatteras.

This was all Horace needed to know and he stopped. Hooking his hammer over his back pocket, he rested his chin on the top rung and let out a combination yodel and sigh. "Damn, that's enough of this shit."

He had covered five windows, and he decided he'd leave the plywood up so Olly May could see what a good husband he was. But all he wanted right then was a cold beer to cool down with. Then he had an even better idea, and after he opened a beer he took an old boat paddle and, with a thick magic marker, he carefully printed out "Olly May's" on the flat part. He nailed the paddle above the front door and stepped back, smiling. Then he wiped his hands on the back of his pants and made himself a thick bologna and lettuce and mustard sandwich on rye bread. After popping open another beer, he sat sideways on the porch swing with his feet up on the armrest, the way he had done since he was a boy, ate the sandwich and began watching the clouds. They were low and ragged now, just above the big oak in his yard, and they were moving faster.

The wind was definitely up. It still looked like a storm and felt like a storm, but now he was convinced that the threat was over.

His two redbone hounds were lying in the shade of the oak and he remembered what his father, who had also been a shrimper, had told him about storms. "Son, don't watch a cat. A cat will sleep through Judgment Day. But a good coon hound can smell one. They can tell you more about a storm than the *Farmer's Almanac*."

Right now the dogs weren't smelling anything. They were sprawled out under the tree in the center of the shade, sound asleep. Molly was sleeping on her back with her back legs spread to keep cool and Rambo was sleeping the way he always slept, with one paw straight out and the other across his face. Then Horace saw Joe Frick across the street on his front porch step.

"Hey, Joe, you want a beer?"

Joe started over. "You talked me into it."

Joe Frick owned a sixty-foot shrimp boat almost identical to Horace's. They tied up at the same pier and worked the same schedules, catching the white shrimp from May to September and the browns from March to June. Joe had been taping his windows when he heard the same report that Horace had heard and he too had stopped. Joe followed Horace into the kitchen. "Man, I'm glad that thing fizzled out."

Horace pulled two beers out of the refrigerator and handed one to Joe. "Anybody heard from Moody and Pete?"

Joe took a long pull on the beer and wiped his mouth with the back of his hand. "They're probably fifty miles upriver by now. I told them this thing wouldn't last."

"I told them the same thing," Horace said. "But you know Moody."

They went back out to the porch, where Horace stretched out on the swing and Joe sat on the top step leaning back on a post in the shade of the big water oak. The tree covered most of the yard, and while the shade from the Spanish moss kept the grass from growing, it was a good place for the dogs to sleep. Off to one side, by the hogwire fence around the collard patch, was a jungle gym, a sandbox, and a swing set that Horace had built for the twins on their fourth birthday, two years ago. Three Dominique hens and a rooster were scratching around for feed under the jungle gym.

Horace and Joe sat for a while drinking their beer and watching a black-and-white cat go slinking down the drainage ditch between the houses and the road. The cat kept low to the ground and kept a wary eye on the dogs, who still hadn't budged. Horace finally spoke. "Whose cat is that, anyway?"

"Damn if I know. He's been hanging around all week. Isn't he long, though?"

Horace stood up and checked his watch. Six o'clock. With his hands on the lower part of his back, he stretched and rotated his shoulders in their sockets.

"That reaching like that really gets me. If I wasn't so damn lazy I'd take me a shower."

But Joe was more interested in the cat. "I bet Jake is feeding him out of the fish house." He stretched out from the step and set the beer can on the rail. "I'm going over to the store. You want anything?"

"No, I'm okay." Horace slung his feet up on the swing arm, pulled his Atlanta Braves cap down low over his eyes, and went to sleep.

6 〜

Where The Ocean Begins

If you fly low over downtown Charleston, you can't help but wonder how a place so small could contain so much history. While the total population of greater Charleston is more than 200,000, in the old city, 20,000 occupy less than six square miles. There, the Historic Charleston Foundation has done what few cities in the world have managed to do—it has saved most of the old houses and kept the skyline almost the way it was in the 1800s. Many streets are still lined with gas lanterns, now electrified, and English cobblestones—sent over as ballast when Charleston was exporting more rice and indigo and cotton than any port in America—that still pave some side streets and can be found beneath the asphalt on the main thoroughfares.

On East Bay Street, Messrs. Walker, Evans, and Cogswell, the oldest printers in the South, still keep their original Confederate money plates in storage. Charlestonians are like this: they hold on to anything old, be it their accents, their furniture, their she-crab soup recipes, even their jokes (the oldest one is that Charleston is where the Ashley and the Cooper rivers come together to form the Atlantic Ocean).

Jokes and she-crab soup aside, it is this holding on to its past that makes Charleston *Charleston*. The old city's motto has always been, "She guards her buildings, her customs, and her laws." If ever a motto fit a city, this one does, for while other cities, with their high rises and endless rows of billboards and fast food franchises, have all come to look almost exactly alike, historic Charleston, by holding on to as much of the past as possible, is today one of the most beautiful cities in the country. Its many church steeples reveal the source of its local nickname, "the Holy City," although the name also might describe the regard many Charlestonians hold for their homes. With its pastel-colored, low skyline, its cobblestone streets and lanterns, the old city can remind you of a village in County Kerry in Ireland, or southern France; or, for the more literary, perhaps the London of the pages of Jane Austen.

Almost as interesting as the city itself are the Charlestonians who inhabit it. There is no one quite like them. They are formidable. Despite earthquakes, hurricanes, and outright poverty and ridicule, the natives there cling to tradition, prejudices, and family names with a desperation that approaches the attention that thoroughbred horse breeders pay to bloodlines. If a young married lady is introducing herself she will admit that she is now a Hampton: "I'm Elizabeth Moultrie Hampton." But then, with a perfectly sensible "south of Broad Street" change of key, she'll quickly add, "wuzza Heyward." By this she is letting you know that there were gardenias and cotillions and better years back in the not-too-long-ago, before she married beneath herself.

In some ways, the people reflect the city; and the city reflects the people. Many of the older houses are held together with massive earthquake bolts running the entire length of the houses, installed after the earthquake in 1886 when the city was too poor to rebuild. Maybe it was then that the old line "too poor to paint, too proud to whitewash" came into being. After that Charleston, which had been the richest city in the country in the eighteenth century due to the rice, indigo, and cotton crops, became one of the poorest. Today, thanks to its naval base and tourism, it's back on its feet and prosperous once again.

One of the more elegant poverty stories, one that has been around for years, concerns a pair of elderly sisters who had fallen on lean times. Despite their circumstances they insisted on telling everyone that they were still summering in Paris. At night they would slip out of their shuttered home and take their constitutional along the Battery, where the historic seawall looks out over Charleston harbor. One night a child recognized them and wanted to rush up and say hello. Her mother held her back, saying, "No, dear, we don't speak to the Tradds in the summertime. They're still in Paris."

Looking south from Marion Square, in the center of the city, is the iron-gray statue of the iron-gray John C. Calhoun. Calhoun took a dim view of early Charleston's wayward ways. In 1807, when smallpox fever was ravaging the town, he called it "a curse for the Charlestonian's intemperance and debaucheries." Calhoun, an Up Country man, championed not only slavery and states' rights, but also temperance, so it's little wonder why the townsfolk of today ignore his grim visage and go on about their business. Calhoun would hardly have approved of the tourism that has gripped the city since the 1960s, and would have been appalled by the camera-strapped outsiders seen padding up and down the narrow streets, peering into backyard gardens and photographing every walking dog and hungry pelican.

Some local wag once said that Charleston could have been invented by Eastman Kodak—everyone seems to arrive in town equipped with a camera, a light meter, and enough film to start a small magazine. They start with a photo of the leather-diapered horses pulling the carriages, then go on to the churches, then the flower ladies, and then each other. As the house tours open in March and the tourists begin arriving with their shorts and sandals and clicking cameras, many of the natives quickly and quietly retreat to their back rooms and their private gardens. Some even leave town until the season is over. And others simply put on their favorite T-shirt: "I Am Not a Tourist—I Happen to Live Here," and go on about their business.

Despite the tourists, most of the old town is about the same

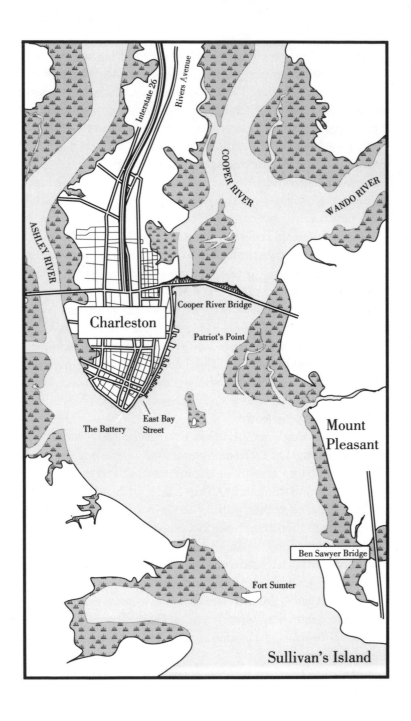

as it was a hundred years ago. The camellias still bloom in November, the azaleas in February, and the magnolia, oleander, and crape myrtle all summer long. Out on the sweeping swamp marsh, amid the expanses of soft, sucking muck known locally as "pluff mud," a great blue heron stands as solitary as he's ever been, and sandpipers still go click, click, clicking along the shallows, eating their microscopic meals. Every year the ospreys faithfully build their nests in the most unlikely places, and the pelicans still look like they will always look— like spectacular drunks rowing their way home with the shrimp boats and the dying sun.

Sunset in Charleston is sensational and one is struck by the incredible variety of roofs and chimney pots and the rainbow of colors they reflect. The houses on East Bay Street and along the Battery facing the ocean, were once owned by ship's captains; many have huge music rooms, aviaries, and rooms big enough for three or four full-sized billiard tables. The woodwork on the porches and eaves of the great houses is delicately carved and presented. With the exception, perhaps, of New Orleans, nowhere in this country are the wrought iron gates, fences, and grave markers more beautiful. Some of the homes have three tiers of porches and, up on top, fenced in with ornamental wrought iron and woodwork, are the widow's walks where the wives and children waved their white scarves and waited.

In the right light the houses on the smaller, narrower streets are out of plumb and tilted forward, sideways, and backward at kindergarten-art angles. Every one is a different crayon color and every doorjamb and roofline seems drawn in by hand. The phone poles and electric lines—in the sections of town where they have yet to be buried—seem to have been set up and strung and hung by children. The fireplugs along the streets look exactly like a child's drawing. It is this innocence, contrasted with the bitter knowledge that slavery and the Civil War started there, that gives Charleston a unique poi-

gnancy that makes it one of the most interesting and picturesque of American cities.

With so much history and so much style, it's easy to see how
one could stand at the Battery flanked by the cannons that
fired out at Fort Sumter, three miles away, and feel almost in-
vulnerable.

Elise was on the phone up in Roscoe and Jay's room, talking to
her mother in Charleston. She was sitting on the very edge of the
bed, trying not to touch anything. Everything was filthy. "Mama,
you can still get over to Galliard." She picked up one of Jay's socks
off his pillow with two fingers. "You sure you don't want to go over
there?"

Elise had to hold the phone away from her ear as Mrs. Derrick
raised her voice and told her that her house was the highest on East
Bay Street and it had already been through more hurricanes than
she could count. From there she rolled into her speech about John
Clements, her husband, and how, when he had been alive, they
had a party during Hurricane Hazel, one of the biggest hurricanes
that had ever struck the coast.

J.C. and Elise's mother, Mary Dubose Derrick, was eighty-two
years old but she was still a power that no one crossed. She had
been born and raised and had had her children in the big house on
East Bay, and her side of the family had produced an ambassador, a
governor, and two U.S. senators. If a stranger didn't know about it,
she didn't hesitate to fill him in on the names, the dates, and the
years in office. Every morning, rain or shine, Mary Dubose walked
from her house all the way to the John C. Calhoun statue up on
Calhoun Street. Charlestonians claimed they could set their clocks
by her, and sometimes when she was trudging through the rain,
people would come out on their balconies and porches and ap-
plaud.

Elise was still holding the phone out at arm's length when J.C. walked in and whispered, "Is she coming?"

Elise covered the speaker and rolled her eyes at the ceiling. "Hell, no. She's absolutely impossible."

J.C. reached for the phone. "Let me talk to her."

But Elise shrugged him away and tried again. "But, Mama, the police will take you right to the door. Everybody's going to be there."

Mrs. Derrick cut her down with a final south of Broad Street remark. "Young lady, I'll have you know I am not everybody."

"Oh, Mama."

"Don't you 'Oh Mama' me. I'm staying right here with my things, and that, Miss Know-It-All, is the long and short of it. I'm hanging up now." And she did.

Elise slammed the phone in the cradle. "She's like a damn mule. What in the hell are we going to do with her?"

J.C. laughed, "Offhand, I'd say nothing. In the meantime, do you think you could help me out here? I've got a house full of people and the kids will be coming in soon."

Before J.C. had even told her what he needed, Elise was downstairs staring into the refrigerator.

J.C. looked in and his spirts dropped. It was as bad as Fanny had said: a few Coca-Colas, a bag of carrots, and a bag of dried-out bagels. There was nothing in the freezer except ice cubes, one can of Minute Maid frozen orange juice, and a half-eaten Popsicle with one of his kids' teeth marks on it.

Elise smiled almost gleefully. "Well, I see you're prepared for just about anything. You're going to have to make a list."

J.C. pulled a brand new yellow legal pad out of a drawer and, holding it like a clipboard, said, "Okay. Shoot."

She pointed her finger as if counting. "We'll start with some eggs."

He wrote: "Eggs, one dozen."

"We'll need more than that with this mob. Better make it two."

She was looking in the crisper in the bottom of the refrigerator. "Mama said she has Dad's shotgun and if any looters come around, or if the police try to make her leave, she'll use it. Can't you just see her with that old thing?"

He smiled as he crossed out one dozen and wrote in two. "That's our Mama."

Elise took the legal pad out of his hand and put it back neatly in the drawer. Then she pulled a long, slim memo pad from her purse. It had bright pink flowers bordering the left side with "THINGS TO DO" written in calligraphy at the top.

"Here, this is much better." She nudged him away. "I'll do this. Okay—eggs, bread, butter, coffee. Then we'll need some peanut butter for the kids and some bacon. J.C., you're going to need everything. You need grease, something to cook with. What in the world are you feeding these kids with around here? Pizza?"

J.C. was now doing nothing but holding the refrigerator door open. "We go out a lot."

Elise went over to the cupboard. "Well, at least you have salt and pepper. And here's some cloves and oregano in case we really want to get fancy. Why don't we just get a dozen Le Menus. We'll cook them in the oven and give the kids milk and soft drinks and the adults can have beer. How's that strike you?"

"Sounds like a feast. Fine with me."

"Hey, where are they, anyway?" she said.

"Football practice. They'll be here around six and they'll be filthy."

J.C. found Elise's organization wearying. If it were up to her, she'd have Roscoe and Jay on such a tight schedule they'd never have any fun. Even now he knew there wouldn't be a single mistake in her shopping list, that the two or three pages she was covering would be in the kind of ornamental cursive handwriting usually reserved for invitations and thank-you letters. But he didn't want to argue. Instead he just let her lecture him on the boys and make her long list. And it was long. It went on and on like a Boy Scout camping list—the only things missing were ropes and hammocks.

"And in case the power goes out," Elise said, "we'll be needing kerosene."

"Jesus!"

"And we'll need lamps and candles and matches."

"Yeah, you already said that. Lamps for the kerosene, and candles in case the lamps go out, and matches in case the candles go out. Now I'm getting the picture." She was still writing up the list when he wrapped his arm around her waist. "But listen, I'm glad you came over. Okay?"

She pulled away. "J.C., what is this cheese doing in the vegetable bin besides stinking? It's hard as a rock." She dropped it in the garbage and without turning she said, "You heard from Beth-Ellen lately?"

"Yeah. She's doing okay with that creep. I think he works on his suntan most of the time." J.C. sighed. "I guess I've let the old place slip a little, huh, Elise? Well, let's get this show on the road and get the stuff."

But Elise had other plans. She sat down with her list and carefully copied out three extra lists. Since there were three cars, three different shopping parties would go out: one to the Piggly Wiggly on Divine, one to the Kroger on Forest Drive, and one to the Food Lion on Harden. Each shopper would call back with the information of how busy the place was, and if the shelves were well stocked. It was also agreed that the shopping teams would be Don and Tracy, Max and Olly May, and J.C. by himself. Roscoe and Jay would be home from football practice right around dark and Elise would remain at the house to meet them.

Back in the living room, Don and Tracy were in the big wing-back chairs, holding hands. The sangria had been too sweet—it tasted like candy. After they'd poured it out in the bathroom, they made themselves vodka tonics. Every time the camera came in close on anything they leaned forward, looking for a shot of the beachfront and listening for news of Sullivan's Island.

"Anything new?" J.C. asked.

"Same old story," Don said. "Nobody knows anything yet."

J.C. checked his watch and switched television stations to the Weather Channel, which was now showing Hugo's leading edge just two hundred miles from the coast. Seventy-five miles back it had wavered almost 90 degrees and started inching north, and at fifty miles it had done the same. But each time it had come back to the northwest course and now it was on that same course again. Only this time it looked like it was staying there.

As J.C. watched the whirling red, blue, and yellow mass, he realized it wasn't like Van Gogh's spinning moons anymore. Now it was more menacing, more terrifying. It looked exactly like a high inside shot of the very center of an atomic blast. A cold chill hit him and he knew there was a good chance of the storm's going right where it was heading. Right for the center of the old city that had been too beautiful for even Sherman to burn—the city where he had been born and raised—the city of Charleston.

J.C. felt his fingers gripping the couch so tight they were stinging. But then he relaxed. He wasn't in Charleston, he was safe in Columbia, 110 miles away. And his boys, Roscoe and Jay, would be home in minutes. His mother was a problem, all right, but she was about as safe as anyone, holed up in her big two-story brick house on East Bay.

Kroger didn't sell kerosene and there wasn't a battery on the shelves or a single can of beer. The only candles were birthday candles, and J.C. dutifully put five dozen packs in the bottom of his cart. Even the distilled water was gone. He bought two large jars of Skippy peanut butter—extra crunchy—four boxes of Nabisco Saltines, and twenty-six cans of assorted Campbell's soups.

He asked a clerk what had been the first thing to go and he smiled and said, "Beer."

J.C. said, "And what was next?"

"Batteries," the clerk said. "You want the third?"

"Yeah."

"Tampax."

J.C. shook his head. "Weird."

It was as if everyone in town had been shopping from Elise's list. Everything was gone or was about to go. All of the frozen Le Menus were gone and Elise was going to have a fit when he brought back a dozen Hungry Man fried chicken dinners with mashed potatoes, creamed corn, and the little apple dumpling desserts with the cherries on top. All the orange juice was sold out, and most of the candy, and so was the Perrier water, which Elise had put three stars by so he wouldn't forget. Instead, he got a six-pack of Gatorade. As he was loading up with pretzels, cheese, and bread, he saw one of the clerks pushing a dolly out of the back, loaded down with Budweiser. He moved in fast and, after piling three twelve-packs in the cart, he headed for the checkout line.

A woman in front was carrying a small portable television set and everyone in the line was trying to watch it. She set it on top of the candy rack and announced to no one in particular, "Here's some news from Charleston. Y'all want to see?"

Everyone crowded in close as the camera came down Meeting Street and stopped at Queen. J.C. could see the green awnings at the Mills House snapping. The few pedestrians out on the street were bent over at hard angles as they headed upwind. Their clothes were plastered skintight to their bodies and their hair was streaming straight back. No one was walking downwind. Palmetto trees were bent low and the strange whistling sound of the wind, picked up even on the small set, was a sound he had never heard before. The camera panned down the street and showed the big window at the bar at 82 Queen, and J.C. checked the faces to see if he knew anyone.

Someone said, "I'll bet that bar is doing some business."

And someone else said, "You can say that again."

The coverage changed to Sullivan's Island and the camera panned out over the water at two surfers who were riding the rolling waves. A policeman on the shore was standing on top of his car waving a red flag and shouting to them over a bullhorn. He wanted them out of the water and off the beach and off the island. But the surfers were too far out and the waves were too big and they were having far, far too much fun.

Someone said, "That's the biggest waves those kids are going to be seeing."

The bag boy said, "Man, would I love to be there."

And someone else said what J.C. was thinking, "Somebody's going to get their butts kicked tonight."

The surfers finally spotted the officer and began dragging their boards in through the surf. J.C. started. For a moment, one of the boys looked exactly like Jay. It was the way he was pushing his hair to the right with his left hand, the little flip he made with his wrist, and the way he waved at the camera. Then he remembered that he and Roscoe were at football practice and they would be home soon, soaking wet and filthy and using up all the clean towels when they showered.

He'd bought them ice cream: Rocky Road for Roscoe, double chocolate fudge for Jay, and he made himself promise to make them sit down right after dinner and do their homework. Once they plugged into television or Nintendo, there wasn't a prayer of them doing anything else.

After checking out, J.C. pushed his cart over to the pay phone by the automatic doors and called Elise. The wind was whipping the colored cartoon section of a newspaper up against the glass as he told her what he'd bought and what he couldn't find. Then he began drumming his fingers on the phone shelf. "Elise, do me a favor and run out to the garage. See if the surfboards are still there. I just got this crazy feeling those kids might be down there in that goddamn surf."

"But you said they were practicing."

"Yeah, I know. But just do it anyway. I'll hold on."

"Okay, I'm going."

He leaned on the phone, waiting for Elise and watching the long lines at the checkout counters. The ten items or less express lines had been converted to regular lines and people were fifteen and twenty deep at each one. The freezer for bagged ice was empty, and from where he was standing he could see whole lines of clean shelves shining in the fluorescent lighting. It was a big night for Kroger.

As he watched a fat lady trying to maneuver two loaded carts out the automatic doors, he tried to remember what Roscoe and Jay had carried out of the house when they left for school that morning. And then it came to him and he relaxed. They'd taken their football gear.

Elise came back to the phone breathing hard. She had been running. "J.C.! They're gone! They're gone! Both of them."

"Damn, are you sure? You looked on the racks, right?"

"Of course I did. I'm not blind. You think they're down there on the beach?"

"I don't know. Listen, I'm leaving right now. I'll be home in a minute."

The very second he hung up he changed his mind. He dropped another quarter in the slot. "Elise, I know this is crazy as hell, but I'm going to Sullivan's Island."

"But, J.C., you can't get through down there. Just come on home, they'll be calling."

"Elise, my mind's made up. I'll leave the groceries with the manager. Get Max to pick them up. I'm sorry, but this is just something I have to do. And, Elise, I want you to do me a favor."

"Sure, J.C. Anything."

"If Beth-Ellen calls, please don't tell her anything about this. Okay?"

"Okay, hon, I can do that."

J.C. drove out of the Kroger parking lot and, picking up Beltline Boulevard, headed for Interstate 26 towards Charleston. As he was waiting for the light to change on Devine, he remembered something. He slammed the steering wheel with his fist. "Damn! Damn!" All shorebound traffic on the interstate had been stopped. He pressed his forehead against the wheel for a minute. "Damn," he said, again. "Okay, now. Think. Think."

He turned right on Blossom and headed for West Columbia. He

passed Maurice Bessinger's Piggie Park Plaza, where the scriptural quote on the fifteen-foot high blinking cross was reading, "The wages of sin are death. . . ." He passed the old Chinese restaurant that Beth-Ellen had liked so much. And then, instead of picking up the interstate at the Waffle House, he continued on down the road on U.S. 176, the Old Charleston Highway.

When Don and Tracy left J.C.'s to go to the Food Lion, they had more on their mind than Elise's shopping list. Buckles, their yellow Labrador, was still out on Sullivan's Island. Instead of going to the Food Lion, they headed straight to K mart, where they made a beeline for the TV center to catch the six o'clock news.

K mart had twelve television sets and every screen was showing Hugo. The news was grim and it was getting grimmer: the leading edge was going to hit Charleston around ten o'clock, with winds of over ninety miles an hour. But that was only a sample of what was to come. Right around midnight the main storm would hit, with winds of up to one hundred and thirty, gusting up to one hundred and fifty. Tornadoes had already been sighted dropping from the clouds and one had touched down near Myrtle Beach.

Ed Carter was on WIS repeating what the other announcers had said earlier. All children and the elderly in the Low Country, from Hilton Head to Myrtle Beach, should be rounded up and taken to the emergency stations. Mobile home dwellers should get out and stay out. They should find a brick house with a basement as far inland as possible. Boat owners that were not at least fifty miles up the rivers should abandon their boats and find shelter. And he emphasized that what might be the worst part of Hugo was the predicted twenty-foot tidal surge that would hit right after the eye had passed.

Tracy and Don sat on the floor in front of a thirty-six-inch television set hoping for some shots of Sullivan's Island and Charleston, but the only thing on the screen was the color satellite picture. The storm had stretched itself into a giant ellipse and was now covering almost everything from Savannah, Georgia, to Wilmington, North

Carolina. In the center was the clear hole of the eye, aimed straight for the Battery.

A strange subdued arrangement of "Margaritaville" was being played over the Muzak system—there was no rhythm, only melody—and all around them people were standing and sitting, while small kids who were tired of watching the storm ran up and down the aisles. Finally an enterprising clerk unwrapped a cartoon video and started it up, and one of the parents bought a four-foot bag of cheese popcorn from aisle twelve. It was a "Blue Light Special."

Most of the crowd seemed to be up from Charleston or over from Myrtle Beach, and they were waiting for news of their homes and their friends and relatives. Many were wondering where they were going to spend the night. Tracy whispered to Don, "Honey, I can't watch any more of this stuff. All I'm doing is worrying about Buckles. I think I'll do a little shopping."

Don groaned. "You just sit here. You've got to stop this. I tell you, he's going to be fine."

"Well, maybe you're right, but I've got to shop. Come on. Get up."

"Nah, you go on. I'll call you if anything happens."

"Okay, I'll be in jewelry."

After Tracy left, WIS stayed on for a few minutes and then cut to the news from the Miami Hurricane Center. Dr. Jim McFadden, their hurricane forecaster, was flying at an altitude of 10,000 feet in the eye wall of the storm, and he sounded excited. Hugo was definitely changing its course and moving north. If it continued to move on out toward Cape Hatteras, Charleston and the entire coast would be spared.

The twenty-five to thirty people sitting and standing around breathed a sigh of relief. Some even cheered. Don jumped up to go get Tracy. After dodging a clutch of children in the aisle, he found her looking at a matching necklace-earrings-bracelet combination that he knew she would buy in the next few minutes and hate the next morning. She already had her credit card out.

"Great news, baby! It looks like Hugo's changing course."

"Are you sure?"

"Damn right, they just announced it."

She pushed the jewelry and her Visa at the clerk. "Oh please, Mr. Hugo, please keep turning."

A woman with a pair of clustered pearl earbobs was standing next to them with her hands folded and her eyes closed. She was praying.

Don said, "Let's get back to the house. I want to see this. Baby, me and you are going to celebrate tonight. God, this is great."

Tracy stopped, "Oh, wait! Look at this. I've just got to have it." She picked up a paisley scarf and tied it around her neck in a big loose knot. Don's heart sank as he recognized it was the same pattern her mother liked, and she was wearing it in the same way her mother wore it. "Honey, you don't want that. Come on," he said, pulling her away.

On the way out Don watched her as she fingered something in each department. They went from the sweaters to the shirts to the slacks—which she almost tried on—to the cameras, past the deli, by the magazines, and finally out the sliding doors. She was pouting because he hadn't let her try on the slacks.

"But, honey," Don said, "we've got to get back and watch this damn thing turn."

"But I thought you said it already turned."

"Oh God, I said it was looking like it was going to turn. Don't you ever listen?"

In the car Tracy turned the radio on. The news was still good, Hugo was still turning north. Andy Thomas, the announcer, was excited but he kept warning that the new direction might not last. The news from Miami, which was relaying what Jim McFadden was reporting from his P-3 Orion "Hurricane Hunter," was that nothing was certain except what was happening at that moment. But as far as he and everyone at the Miami Center could tell, it looked like it was going back out to sea.

Tracy said, "Will you please tell me why they can't predict anything more than five or ten minutes ahead? Hell, I can do that. Oh, I hope Buckles can get in through that hole in the cellar. Lord, I hope that fool's okay."

"He's fine, sugarplum. I'll bet he's already got himself a gal he's going to spend the night with."

"**D**id you hear it? Did you hear the news?" Tracy shouted, as she and Don came rushing in the door. "Hugo's turning north. It's going back to sea."

Elise was smiling. She knew. Roscoe had just called: he and his friend Mike were safe out at Don's house with Buckles. She had gone to Kroger's and picked up the groceries and was now storing the food on the shelves in the cupboards and the refrigerator. Max and Olly May were still out shopping.

Don kissed Tracy's cheek. "Didn't I tell you he was going to make it?"

She said, "Yes, you did. Now all you got to do is promise me and guarantee that Hugo's going to keep on turning. Now say it."

Don grinned and went through their old ritual. "I promise and I guarantee it."

Tracy shook her head. "No, say it right. Say it all."

Don hugged her. "Okay, I promise and I guarantee that Hurricane Hugo is going to turn off to Cape Hatteras and it's going to miss Charleston."

Don mixed himself a fresh drink and carried it out the back door. The magnolia leaves hadn't been raked in weeks and he shoved the ones around the doorstep aside with his foot. The wind seemed to be down and to the west the sky was clear and the stars were out. In the distance he heard the deep horn of the CSX train rumbling through town. There was the smell of woodsmoke in the air, or maybe it was diesel smoke from the train. It didn't look like hurricane weather and it didn't feel like it. Maybe it would keep on turning and he'd be back out on Sullivan's Island by tomorrow, casting for the stripers that were beginning to run.

Max and Olly May barged into the house loaded down with groceries and a case of Miller High Life.

Max was shouting. "Y'all hear the news? Hugo's heading for the Cape!" Then, as he set the bags on the kitchen table, he grinned. "Which, if I remember correctly, is precisely what I predicted."

7 〜

September: Remember

With the exception of largely futile experimentation with dry ice and silver iodide to prevent hurricanes—by making them discharge their energy in the form of rain—there has been to this day no way of stopping, or even affecting, the development of a killer storm. All we can do is get out of the way.

Getting out of the way, however, has not always been an easy matter. Here is the account of one admiral who could *not*:

> Eyes never beheld the seas so high, angry and covered by foam. The wind not only prevented our progress but offered no opportunity to run behind any headland for shelter; hence we were forced to keep out in the bloody ocean, seething like a pot on a hot fire. Never did the sky look more terrible; for one whole day and night it blazed like a furnace; the flashes came with such fury and frightfulness that we all thought the ships would be blasted. All this time the water never ceased to fall from the sky. I don't say, "it rained," because it was like another Deluge. . . .

This might have been written in 1991 during the most recent Bay of Bengal disaster, or during Hugo on the night of September 21, 1989, but in fact it was written five centuries ago and the admiral who wrote it was Christopher Columbus.

The West Indies have, of course, been mauled by hurricanes since long before Columbus's account, but the natives, having no written language, left no records. They have, however, left proverbs and sayings; one handed down from the slaves in the Bahamas became a calypso jingle:

June: too soon
July: stand by
August: look out you must
September: remember
October: all over

None of the early accounts of hurricanes and typhoons give the details of the number of lives lost and the damage. Not only were records sketchy, there wasn't very much for a hurricane to damage except for trees.

In 1772 a killer storm hit the city of St. Croix in the Virgin Islands and a fifteen-year-old boy wrote a letter about it to his father on another island:

> Great God! What horror and destruction—it is impossible for me to describe or you to form any idea of it. The roaring of the sea and wind-fiery meteors flying about in the air—the prodigious glare of almost perpetual lightning—the crash of the falling houses—and the ear-piercing shrieks of the distressed were sufficient to strike astonishment into Angels . . .

The boy's father had the letter published in the *St. Croix Gazette* and the quality of the writing so impressed the readers that they collected a fund to send him to college in New York City. The boy was a brilliant student, and within five years he became confidential secretary to General George Washington. From there he rose to become one of the authors of the Constitution and might have even become president, except he was disqualified for the office by not having been born in the United States. His name was Alexander Hamilton.

But a letter from Miss Corrie Dusenbury, who lived in Woodland, South Carolina, perhaps offers a much calmer and more sensible view of what one should do in a hurricane. She remembers the storm of October 13, 1893, as follows:

> Papa, a businessman, had gone to Georgetown that day and had left Mama in charge with the help of a hired man

named Zack. When Zack came running up to Mama and said the waves had risen over the creek bank and were headed toward the house, she responded, with no emotion at all in her voice, "Place the flour barrel on the stove and all lower dresser drawers on the bed."

After Zack had done this, he ran to the front door to bolt it. "Don't lock the door," Mama said quietly, "open the door so when the water reaches it, it won't break the door down." It was Mama's lack of alarm that kept the children from becoming anxious. As long as she went about and spoke with such composure, we were not afraid. Mama called to the children and informed us that we should find a place on the stairs to sit. "Take the dog with you," she said, "and don't sit on a step too near the top nor too near the bottom."

As we sat there, the water came through the house with many things bobbing up and down, including some white chickens.

Once in a while a little knowledge, such as opening the windows on the lee side of a hurricane and then remembering to reverse the procedure when the storm swings around, has saved homes. Tornadoes are another story, for with a tornado there is virtually no warning and all you can do is keep as low as possible. During a hurricane, tens, hundreds, even thousands of tornadoes are spawned and spun off the edges. They travel at an average speed of forty-five miles an hour and, with luck, can be outrun in a car. They travel from the southwest toward the northeast, and can be both strong enough to lift a locomotive and gentle enough to move a cow a thousand yards and set it down without a scratch.

Some of what we know of tornadoes has come to us at considerable cost. For years midwestern Baptists and Methodists wrestled with the moral dilemma of why tornadoes destroyed almost every church in the towns they struck but left untouched the blaspheming saloons. The answer came late, but it eventually came, when a heavy-drinking sage announced that the close-minded churches closed and bolted their doors to the visiting storm, thereby creating a vacuum, while saloons, traditionally more open-minded, had the good sense to keep theirs open.

Gary Jennings, in his book *The Killer Storms,* tells us that the author of *The Wizard of Oz,* L. Frank Baum,

> was apparently aware of the big tornado that struck Irving, Kansas, in 1879. That storm first lifted a large iron bridge off the Blue River and wadded it up like a piece of tinfoil, then went on to mash the town of Irving as flat as the corn fields around it. The few families in the area who lived through the devastation were so terrorized that for weeks afterward they never went to bed at the same time, but kept someone awake and on watch in each house, to cry a warning if another storm would come.

The word "tornado" is derived from two Spanish words, one meaning "turning" and the other "thunderstorm." Out on the Great Plains, which seems to be the area in the world they hit the most, they are called twisters. Tornadoes have also struck London and Moscow; they have probably struck every country located in a temperate zone.

Jennings goes on to describe how a tornado differs from a hurricane:

> To understand how the tornado differs from them, imagine that a hurricane is squeezed, to compress both its bulk and its energy. The 20-mile-wide eye becomes no bigger around than, say, a city block. The air that has been briskly rising through the eye's broad chimney will now be literally whistling up this constricted tube.

Survivors of tornadoes who have actually seen inside the twisting cone tell us that the entire interior is lit up by lightning bolts. Since each bolt of lightning causes a clap of thunder, and since the lightning is continuous, the sound that a tornado makes, often reported as like that of a passing train, is in reality the sound of endlessly booming thunder.

Gary Jennings also reports that at one time or another, a tornado has:

Impaled fragile, brittle straws deep in tree trunks and fence posts, as if they had been sharp and sturdy spears.

Sheared the wool off a whole herd of sheep, but left the denuded sheep grazing unperturbed and unharmed.

Scooped up a prairie pond, carried it for miles, and dumped onto a bewildered town its contents of several hundred frogs.

Picked up a 700-pound refrigerator and carried it for three miles before dropping it.

Pelted a farmer with sand and grit, as if by a shotgun, so that he wore the tattoo of it embedded in his skin all the rest of his life.

Carried a whole herd of steers flying though the air over Kansas, where they looked, said an observer, "like a flight of gigantic birds."

Popped a full-grown rooster inside a narrow-necked two-gallon jug, alive and without a feather ruffled.

Finally, Mr. Jennings tells us of a cookies-and-milk ending that happened in 1955 at Bowdle, South Dakota, where a mother watched from a window while her nine-year-old daughter rode her pony in a field next to the house. "Suddenly the pony, with the little girl still astride, shot high into the air. The mother dashed outdoors, but soon lost sight of the pair, as they were blown fully a half mile away. But the child was still in the saddle when the pony was set down; she suffered only a couple of minor bruises and the pony was not hurt at all."

Once J.C. was out of the city limits and on the open road he kept the speedometer on eighty. The radio was on and every time a report came in on Hugo, he slowed to make sure he heard it all. He'd been on the road less than thirty minutes and was twenty miles south of St. Matthews when he heard the news that Hugo was shifting to the north. He pulled off the road and onto the shoulder and, in a combination of exhaustion and complete relief, he slumped over the wheel and said, "Thank you, Jesus."

J.C. pulled into an old-fashioned gas station and general store that had a wooden canopy hanging out over the Gulf pumps. After he filled the tank, he leaned on the counter with two locals and watched Hugo's progress on the television mounted on the wall. One of the men laughed, "I told you it would bend off. Hell, they've been doing that since I started planting soybeans."

The owner handed J.C. his change. "Anything else?"

"No, that'll do it." Then he changed his mind. "Yeah, give me a Bud. I've got a little celebrating to do. I got two kids out there on Sullivan's Island."

The owner slid him his beer and pushed his money back to him. "Mister, let me buy this one. Don't you know it would have been rough out there if that thing had hit. Are you driving on down?"

"No, you know kids. Hell, they'd skin me alive if I showed up now." He laughed and slapped both hands on the counter. "Now you talk about somebody that's relieved, you people are looking at him. Hell, let me buy y'all a beer."

One of the men laughed. "Sure thing. We'll drink with you. Clayton's the name. Sam Clayton. And this old drunk's Bud Renfrow."

J.C. finished off his first beer, opened a second, and stayed glued to the television. He breathed easier now and he quietly thanked the Lord again for nudging the storm north. Then he began thinking of how wild it must have been for the boys to ride the big waves. A part of him was proud that they weren't afraid of trying it. But another part wanted to spread-eagle them over a chair and whip their butts until their ears rang.

He looked around the old general store for something to buy to take back to Elise and Max and the others. Hanging from wooden pegs on the big six-by-six beams that crossed the ceiling were mule collars, fan belts, plowshares, and even sugar-cured hams. The stock looked like it had been there for a hundred years, and he could smell the brine from the pickle barrel. It reminded him of the place where his Dad would buy bait when they went fishing down on the Edisto. A long bench that was slick with wear sat out front between the gas pumps with a red-and-black checkerboard painted in the center seat. Initials had been cut on the edges to keep track of old bets and old scores. Except for the television, the prices, and the new brand names, the place looked like it was stuck in 1960; it even had an old-fashioned curved glass candy case.

J.C. bought a ham and four pounds of hoop cheese and, unable to resist the pickle brine smell, twelve cucumber-sized pickles. The owner fished out a recipe from his cash register on how to prepare the ham to get some of the salt out. "Of course, I like that salt myself. I like it just fine. If you just slice it thin and fry it in fresh grease, you can't beat it with a stick."

For some reason, listening to the man talk about the ham made him realize what a terrible father he was. He couldn't remember the last time he'd taken Roscoe and Jay fishing, or anything, and he never punished them. Well, this time he would take a firm stand and cuss them out and ground them for at least a week. They wouldn't be able to talk him out of this one. He would pull the plug on the television and the radio and he'd make them sit in their rooms and study. And there would be no outgoing calls on the phone. Underline that, *none*! Hell, maybe they could do some yard-work for a change. But after J.C. had worked out the weekend schedule, he caught himself smiling in the mirror behind the counter. They had actually surfed in those big waves out at Sullivan's and had been on television. And there was no question about it, they would look at him the way they always looked at him and talk him right out of any punishment.

J.C. decided that since the boys were safe, he would drive on in to Charleston and see his mother. He would also be able to check up on the kids and find out just what had happened. But first he would call Elise. The store owner told him to come behind the counter to use the phone. J.C. thanked him and dialed his house. When Elise answered, he asked her if she'd heard anything.

Elise said, "Well, J.C., you were right. That was them out on Sullivan's. Can you believe it? Thank God that thing turned off, they could have been in real trouble out there."

She told him that Roscoe and Mike had called in from Don and Tracy's and that Jay and Bill had been picked up by the police. The dog, whose name she'd forgotten, was safe, and Tracy had finally shut up about him. An operator had helped Olly May get through to her children at a shelter, but not to her husband. Then Elise added, "Oh, J.C., I'm so glad it turned. Do you have any idea of what might have happened?"

J.C. nodded, "I sure do. Listen, I'm going to drive on in and see Mama. Hey, give me Don's number on the island. I want to call Roscoe."

She read it off to him and then added, "Now, don't be too hard on him. I'm sure he was scared to death out there."

He hung up and dialed Don's house. The phone rang only once before Roscoe picked it up.

J.C. said, "Hey, Bub. It's me. Everything okay out there?"

Roscoe had to raise his voice over the screaming wind. "Not exactly. I think we made a big mistake coming out here."

J.C. knew he had to be firm. "Let's call it three mistakes. Number one, you skipped school. Number two, you shouldn't be down there in the first place. And number three, you should have called the police. Oh, yeah, and number four, I guess you know you're breaking the damn law? That place is supposed to be evacuated."

"Sorry, Dad. I guess we just got carried away. But you ought to see the water out here now, it's up over the dunes and it's up under the house." Roscoe hesitated. "Dad, I'm beginning to get scared. What should we do if it starts leaking?"

J.C. knew he was being set up. They wanted sympathy.

"Just stick some paper towels under the door. That ought to do it. Okay, let's cut this out. You got a pencil?"

"Yeah, I just saw one. Yeah, here it is."

"Okay, write this number down. It's your grandmother's. I know you've got it, but I want you to write it down anyway." He read off the number, twice. "All right, you got that? I'll be there and I want you to call me in about an hour. Okay?"

"Yessir, I'll do that. And Dad?"

"Yeah, Bub."

"You aren't mad at us, are you?"

"Naw, you know me, Old Mr. Softie. Hell, I'd of probably done the same thing myself. All right, now don't forget to call me."

"Okay, Dad. I love you."

"Same here, Bub. I love you too."

As J.C. drove on south of Holly Hill he started to watch an enormous low cloud with a black and purple bottom sliding across a soybean field. The bottom looked like a big turnip lying on its side, and it seemed to be pulsing. At first, J.C. thought it was his imagination. He pulled off the shoulder and stopped. It was not his imagination. He was petrified. Everything in him told him to turn around and drive in the opposite direction as fast as he could, but he sat there spellbound, drawn to it like a chicken to a chicken snake.

J.C. watched as the turnip shape turned and began standing on its end and reaching out with a long finger to touch the ground. It was as if it were testing the area to see if it were the right place, the right temperature, the right something. The tip seemed no bigger than his car as it touched down, and as it did, it pulled the shape away clean from the cloud. Now it was free, being driven by some inner wind. It had a life of its own; it looked like a ragged drunk, wobbling back and forth in the soybeans, trying to decide what to do and where to go. Suddenly, and for what seemed like no reason, it lurched forward and began moving off to his right.

J.C. Derrick was thirty-nine years old and had lived all his life in South Carolina without ever seeing a tornado. Now, as he watched it heading for an old tobacco barn, he caught himself hoping it would hit. He didn't know why, he just wanted to see it happen.

Because of golf, J.C. was good with distances, and he knew that the tornado stayed on the ground for about one hundred yards before it pulled back up for another two hundred. Like a kite with not enough tail, it wouldn't stay up and it wouldn't stay down.

And then there it was. J.C.'s wish came true. The tornado touched down about fifty yards from the tobacco barn and was heading straight for it. Just as it was about to hit, it began pulling up again. Only the tail clipped the barn, and that only lightly, but it was enough. The roof went whirling straight up, the walls followed, and every lath and beam and plank and shred of ancient tobacco went corkscrewing and swirling up into the lunatic funnel. He'd never seen such effortless power, he'd never heard such an incredible roar. His big Buick was shaking as if the earth was opening up beneath it. Then he saw that the barn had vanished. Nothing was left except two long leaves of tobacco that were slowly spiraling back to the ground as the tornado moved on across the soybeans, skirted the woods, and then pulled back up into the cloud.

PART TWO

Thursday Night

8

Storm Surge

The day Hurricane Hugo came ashore in South Carolina, 40-mph winds began whipping across the Low Country first thing in the morning. Even though Hugo was still more than 300 miles away, a strange feeling was in the air that this one might be different. This one might hit Charleston head-on. Early that morning police began ordering everyone to leave the sea islands along the coast—Kiawah, Seabrook, Edisto, James Island, Hilton Head, the Isle of Palms, and Sullivan's Island. By noon, people along the entire coast from Daufuski, at the tip of Hilton Head, all the way up to Myrtle Beach, were beginning to clear out. A full evacuation was under way and Interstate 26 from Charleston to Columbia and Interstate 20 from Florence and Myrtle Beach to Columbia were packed with cars heading inland.

The stores were swamped with customers buying batteries, bottled water, canned goods, flashlights, and candles, and almost everyone else was glued to their television sets. Probably at no other time in modern history has there been a more vivid demonstration of the power of television and the dependency that our society has on it. For with television, people were able to see exactly what Hugo was and what it was doing. They were able to see if they and their family and friends were in danger, and to find out exactly what precautions they should take. Without television there would have been hundreds of casualties, maybe even thousands. The first thing some people did when the electricity went out was to run extension cords across the street from the homes of their neighbors who had power so they could use not their refrigerators or their lights, but their television sets.

By 9 P.M. there was no doubt about it: Hugo was heading straight for Charleston. Mayor Joseph Riley, who would ride out the night at City Hall, announced, "All we can do now is pray, and hope that all the precautions we have taken will be sufficient." Right after his announcement the wind increased and the clock in the steeple of St. Michael's Episcopal Church stopped.

During the next hour all hell broke loose in the Holy City as gas lines broke, high voltage wires sparked and flashed, and explosions rocked Charleston from the Battery all the way across the Cooper River Bridge to Mt. Pleasant. Added to the sound of the ravaging wind and the gas line blasts was another sound. Electrical transformers on the tops of the telephone poles were blowing out. The sky, which had turned to a strange sickly green, was now studded with brilliant white phosphorescent flashes, and to anyone out on the street or peering out a window, it must have looked like the bombing of Baghdad did two years later—or the end of the world. And all of this was happening while the brunt of the storm was almost two hours away.

By 11 P.M. Hugo was ashore and following the grinding path of destruction that would devastate Charleston and the Low Country; go through Sumter, Camden, and Florence 100 miles away; hit Charlotte, North Carolina, 200 miles away; wind through parts of Virginia, West Virginia, and Pennsylvania; and keep on going until the storm finally ran out of steam across the Canadian border.

No one has ever successfully measured, or probably will ever successfully measure, the power of a hurricane. The force has been compared to that of a volcano, an earthquake, a tidal wave. One scholar reported that if you dropped a dozen hydrogen bombs in the path of a Category Four storm, it would be like hitting an elephant with a BB gun. While it's true the winds in tornadoes are stronger and more concentrated than those of hurricanes, and they do more damage where they hit, the range of a tornado rarely exceeds more than fifty or sixty miles, and follows a narrow path. But the winds of a full-fledged hurricane can cover hundreds, even thousands of miles, can reach speeds of 200 mph, and can last from two to three days to a week.

One unnamed storm still stands out in the record book. It started in mid-August over West Africa, moved across the Atlantic, slid along the outer islands of the West Indies, and then followed the curve of the United States up to New York. All this time, fortunately, it stayed at least 200 miles out to sea. When it was opposite New York it swung east and headed back across the Atlantic for Europe, where it crossed Norway and Sweden and the northern reaches of Russia and finally dissipated over the Arctic Ocean. It had lived for over a month, becoming for a while a mature Category Four hurricane, and had traveled more than 15,000 miles.

Scientists who work with hurricanes tell us that since the main ingredients for powering a hurricane are the sun and warm water, and since the sun's power is inexhaustible, they have every reason to believe that, theoretically, a hurricane, under the right conditions, could very well last indefinitely.

The raw power that a Category Four hurricane unleashes in a single day would, if converted into electricity, be enough to run all of the electrical equipment, motors, generators, and household appliances in the entire United States for more than six months. Another way of putting it is that the energy, unleashed, is greater than that of eighty earthquakes of the size and magnitude that destroyed San Francisco in 1906.

While the scientists disagree on many things—what triggers a hurricane to begin with, what causes the spin that is put on the initial winds, and how the chimney in the center exhausts itself at the top—they do agree that a majority of the storms that reach North America and do the most damage begin roughly about 300 miles off the western shore of Africa in the area of the Cape Verde Islands. When they begin there they have an uninterrupted stretch of 2,500 miles of tropical ocean to travel over and pick up energy.

The typhoon of the Pacific Ocean and the cyclone of the Indian Ocean are identical to the Atlantic hurricane, except that those which form in the Southern Hemisphere spin in the opposite direction. And they are often stronger because they can travel over an even larger area of warm water. Wind speeds have been reported to exceed 250 miles an hour, which was what happened in 1737 when the fabled cyclone struck the Bay of Bengal near present-day Bangladesh. The bay narrows down to a V as it gets close to the delta of the Ganges River, and it was into these narrows that the cyclone whirled. It kept gaining speed and force, pushing a mass of water before it until, when it hit the land, the storm surge had risen to the incredible height of more than 100 feet. In minutes it destroyed more than 20,000 vessels and the entire port and city at the river's mouth, and killed 300,000 people.

While the entire coastline of South Carolina is only 200 miles long, in some ways the structure of the bays and estuaries that open onto the Atlantic can function, though on a much smaller scale, like the V of the Bay of Bengal. As a storm surge flows into the mouth of each bay, it starts building and moving faster where the shoreline tapers into a funnel shape. A ten-foot surge in the ocean can very quickly rise to fifteen feet, twenty feet, and even higher. If there happens to be a high tide, it can rise even more. A ten-foot surge, coming at a time when there is a ten-foot high tide, will become a twenty-foot surge.

When Hugo made landfall in Charleston around 11:30 P.M., the storm surge coming in was around thirteen feet. Hugo's winds, above 135 mph and gusting to 150, drove it right over the seawall at the Battery and into almost every house downtown.

At least 80 percent of the buildings in the city were damaged, and City Hall lost more than half its roof. Folly Beach, on the coast a few miles southeast of the Battery, lost 80 percent of its homes, and its main roads were stripped completely bare of pavement. The famous Atlantic House Restaurant, which had been through several hurricanes, was completely destroyed; only a few pilings were left.

A twenty-foot tidal surge at Sullivan's Island took out most of the front row of beach houses; the Ben Sawyer Bridge to the mainland was put out of commission for two weeks. One end of the bridge was forced down into the water, while the other end was left pointing to the sky. The nearby Isle of Palms lost its fishing pier and more than ninety homes, and one hundred boats were stacked up on top of the houses like cordwood. Every fishing pier from the Isle of Palms to Myrtle Beach, over one hundred miles north, was completely destroyed. Pawley's Island was cut in two by Hugo, and a new hundred-foot-wide channel appeared where several homes once stood.

As the surge funneled into the Wando, Cooper, and Ashley rivers around Charleston, hundreds of boats were swept upstream and demolished. Brian and Kathleen Jackson of Fort Lauderdale, Florida, died when their anchored catamaran turned over in the Wando. Paul Spencer died trying to save his thirty-foot powerboat thirty miles up the Cooper. Robert Page and Harold Hutson tried to ride out the storm in their shrimp boat in the Wando and were killed when their boat was slammed against the S.C. Route 41 bridge, which crosses the river a few miles north of Charleston.

On up the coast, from McClellanville to Georgetown to Murrell's Inlet, it was the same story. The small fishing village of Awendaw was almost washed away by a twenty-foot tidal surge and the Awendaw Creek bridge on U.S. 17 collapsed.

McClellanville, a tiny village of 600 two miles across the marsh from the Atlantic Ocean, was one of the hardest hit areas in the state. The town was completely cut off from the outside world by massive flooding; the entire population huddled together, trapped in six to seven feet of water, inside the Lincoln High School shelter. Outside the school, cars and boats were stacked up five and six deep in the water, and of the twenty-eight boats anchored at the village dock, only three made it through the storm.

Around 7:30, not long after the good news that Hugo was turning north came from CNN and the Miami weather station, the bad news came into J.C. Derrick's living room. It came from Miami, from the "Hurricane Hunter" plane that was flying along in the eye of the storm. It was simple and straightforward. Hugo had stopped turning north. It had veered sharply back to the left, and was now back on its old course, bearing 270 degrees, heading directly for the South Carolina coast, straight for Charleston.

Max cursed and Don groaned. Tracy just sat there with her mouth open, unable to speak, and Olly May began to cry. She still hadn't heard from Horace. Elise went rigid thinking about Roscoe and Mike out on Sullivan's Island. She took a deep breath, stood up, and as if she were sleepwalking, headed for the phone in Roscoe's bedroom. She could have used the kitchen phone, but she felt she wanted to be alone when she tried to tell him what to do. As she dialed, she figured out that he'd probably heard the news on television; she had no idea what she would tell him. The phone didn't ring. She hung up and dialed again. Once again it didn't ring. She dialed the operator and told her the problem. "It's a real emergency, Miss. Can you give me a hand here?"

The operator said, "I don't know what to tell you. That number is out on Sullivan's Island and I'm afraid those lines have just gone down. There's no way to get through."

"But you have to. I've got to talk to them."

"Oh, honey, I'm just so sorry. But there's really nothing I can do

right now. Try the Charleston police, they might be able to help
you. They'll be pretty busy, but keep trying, you'll get through."

Elise hung up and started calling the police department. The operator was right, the lines were busy. She hung up, got herself comfortable, and started the long process of dialing again and again and
again.

Back in the living room, Max put his arm around Olly May.
"Come on, now. I bet Horace has that boat and that house of yours
so battened down and so tight nothing can touch it. You take it easy
now, he's going to take care of everything."

Olly May was biting her bottom lip and trying to keep from
crying. "If I could have just talked to him. He doesn't know where I
am or anything." She stood up, and, clenching her hands together,
she began pacing.

Suddenly the CNN picture turned to static. Max picked up the
remote control and began flipping through the channels. "Great.
Just great. No more TV."

Olly May wiped her eyes and moved over. "Let me try a second."
She opened a panel at the bottom of the screen, turned a couple of
knobs, and pushed the remote to Channel 10. The picture came up,
and there before them was Joe Pinner.

Olly May was still drying her eyes. "If that ever happens again,
just push the cable-ready button off and pretend like you don't have
cable anymore. It works every time."

They all sat there, petrified, watching Hugo moving in on the
coast. They could do nothing but watch. Even Max was silent.
There was no doubt about it, it was definitely going to hit right in
the center of Charleston. A few minutes before nine, WIS began
flashing a red storm alert, warning Columbians of high winds,
heavy hail, terrible road conditions, and possible tornadoes. The
police chief came on, telling all motorists to stay off the roads until
the warning was over. He suggested that everyone keep their radio
or television on, as there would be updates as the night progressed.
As he was talking about the danger of falling trees and broken high

voltage lines, the lights in J.C.'s house went out, then came back on again. The wind began shaking the shutters and somewhere, not too far away, a siren was wailing. It wasn't much different from a strong thunderstorm, but for some reason it seemed a lot worse.

J.C. heard the news of Hugo turning back toward Charleston as he was driving down Rivers Avenue through Hanahan in the pouring rain. He stopped at a phone outside a Magic Mart, and, pulling his Wildwood golf cap down low to shield his face, he turned his back to the pounding rain and dialed the beach house. At first he thought he'd dialed wrong, but when he couldn't get through the second time he began suspecting the worst. The wind was surging and gusting and tiny hail the size of BB's was rattling on the booth as he dialed O and asked the operator for some help. But he got the same news Elise had gotten just minutes before; the lines were down on Sullivan's Island. He hung up, dizzy, and quickly sat down on the curb. His knees were trembling and he could taste the salty rain. He ignored the stinging hail. All he could think about was that Roscoe was trapped, the tidal wave would wash right over him and there was nothing he could do. It was all he could do to keep from getting sick as he sat there with the rain and the hail slashing across his face.

About a hundred feet of electric wire began rising in the air like a giant snake in front of a Coca-Cola sign. J.C. watched it as it began to whip back and forth, knowing that if it came near him it could take his head off cleaner than a shark bite. But still he sat there. Limbs were snapping off the trees and a Hurby Kurby garbage container came tumbling down the sidewalk and slammed into the phone booth a few feet away. When the Rivers Avenue sign blew off and crashed in the street in front of him, he climbed back in the Buick and headed for his mother's house. J.C. drove slowly down Rivers Avenue, dodging fallen branches, garbage cans and whole billboards in the road. Maybe, by some miracle, Roscoe had been able to make it to his grandmother's house after all. But as he watched a big Camel cigarette sign buckle and begin to come apart, he knew he was fooling himself. It was almost eight o'clock, and the full force of Hugo would hit the coast in less than three hours.

Mary Dubose Derrick was pleased when J.C. arrived, but she was shocked when she heard the news that Roscoe was out on Sullivan's Island. "How on earth did you let something like this happen? I've never heard of such a thing." The rain, driven by the wind, was leaking in under the doors and windows, and she was busy stuffing the cracks with napkins and towels.

The lights had gone out at nine and Mary Dubose had a line of candles burning on the coffee table in front of her living room couch. For the moment, J.C. was thankful that it was candlelight and she couldn't see his eyes. "Mama, for God's sake, ease up."

But Mary Dubose was not about to ease up. She began lecturing him on the responsibility of being a father as she folded a towel lengthwise and jammed it into the crack under a door. But J.C. wasn't listening, he was staring into the candles' light and going back over everything he'd said to Roscoe on the phone. Everything had been brusque, and he hated himself for not being more careful. He remembered calling him Bub at the end. That was good, that was what he used to call him when he was little. But that was the only nice thing he'd said.

He tried to imagine what was going on out on the island, but nothing came but a terrifying view of waves crashing onto the beach and streaming across the dunes for the house. The announcers on his mother's portable radio were now saying that the island was where they were predicting the tidal surge would hit the hardest. Any house that wasn't at least sixteen feet aboveground would probably be washed away. J.C. squeezed his left fist in his right hand trying to figure out how high Don and Tracy's was. He remembered parking underneath but he couldn't remember how high it was from the top of his car to the flooring. Was it ten feet, twelve feet? But maybe it was only eight.

He knew he had to keep busy and he forced himself to get up

and help his mother with the wet towels. He'd wring them out in the tub, and hand them to her, and she'd jam them in under the windows and the doors. Later, when he got a chance, he took two candles and went down to the basement. After tearing some plywood from a packing case, he brought it upstairs and began nailing it over a crack in the window molding where the wind was hissing through. As he drove the first nail in, Mary Dubose said, "Now don't go ruining everything."

"Mama, for God's sake, if I don't seal this thing up the whole damn thing's going to blow."

She huffed, "Well, young man, you needn't get so snappy. There's just no need to be so destructive."

As J.C. worked at the window he saw a huge shadow loom and then pass in front of the house. A heavy sound reverberated and he felt the house shake. Then he heard glass breaking in the kitchen. A huge limb from a live oak had fallen next door and had crushed a Chevrolet almost flat to the ground. And then, as if some strange kind of rhythm were taking over, lightning flashed and two more big limbs fell. In the flash he saw the water had risen above the seawall and was rolling down East Bay Street. All hell was breaking loose, but it was like it was happening to someone else: none of it seemed to touch him. All he could think about was his Roscoe, and all he could do was pray that somehow he was safe out on that dark and lonely island.

Roscoe, still thinking that Hugo had turned off and was now on its way to Cape Hatteras, laid out four slices of bread on the butcher-block kitchen table, and spread them thick with peanut butter. The refrigerator was packed with beer and, after pulling out two cans of Heineken and popping them open, he handed one to Mike. "Here you go, stud. Food for a king."

Mike was in front of the big picture window, shining the light out into the surf. "Damn, look at it. It's getting higher."

Roscoe bit into his sandwich. "You think so? Hell, that's not so much."

"God, Roscoe, how can you be so dumb? Look how high it is on that stupid sign."

Roscoe, who was sitting cross-legged, Indian style, on the floor in front of the window, kept chewing, and when Buckles came over he gave him half his sandwich. "I wish we had a tide chart. It's got to be high tide causing most of this."

Mike was sounding more and more worried. "High tide, my ass. Who in the hell told you the storm turned?"

"Elise, my damn aunt, that's who. She saw it on the report from Miami. Said it was heading for Cape Hatteras."

"You swear?"

"I swear. Now be cool, man. You got to stop being so spooked."

Buckles was making a yawning overbite, trying to get the peanut butter off the roof of his mouth, and Roscoe was laughing. "Hey, take a look at this. It always kills me."

Mike laughed, but only for a second. "Maybe that thing turned back. It looks terrible out there." He handed Roscoe the light. "Look where it is on the sign now."

Roscoe, who was now lying on his back, played the flashlight beam over the seashells and starfish on the fishnet covering the ceiling. "Don't be stupid. You take a high tide plus a storm behind it and anything can happen."

"Well, anything is. Something just jumped out there. I swear it."

Roscoe rolled over and cupped the flashlight against the window to focus it. But he didn't have to. Lightning was filling the sky and he could see that the Century 21 sign had sunk from sight. The wind was stronger and a new and much lower howling was coming from under the house.

Mike tried to joke but his voice sounded strangled and far away. "Well, we sure as hell have the beach to ourselves."

Now Roscoe was the quiet one as he watched the spot where the sign had disappeared. There was no trace of it, and he could feel in his fingertips and the back of his neck that under the house the water was getting deeper. Buckles had squeezed in under the coffee table and his ears were laid back flat on his head. He was looking worried as his eyes went from Roscoe to Mike and then back to Roscoe.

Mike said, "Don't laugh, man, but I got to tell you something. I'm scared."

Roscoe hesitated, then he said it. "Yeah, me too." He punched Mike lightly on the shoulder. "But you know something? I'm glad I'm doing this with you. Jay or Billy would've been flipping me out by now."

Mike's voice was sounding thin and dry. "Roscoe, there's something I've got to say. I lied about Cindy Murdock. We didn't do a thing but watch old movies."

Roscoe shrugged. "I knew that."

Mike looked over. "How? Who told you?"

"Aw, man, nobody told me. It's the same damn thing with me. All I've done is talk about it."

The lightning was flashing faster and faster and the sky was turning from red to green and then back to red. "Roscoe?"

"Yeah, Mike?"

"Man, I just hope I get to do it before I die."

The house shuddered and the walls were flexing in and out as if they were breathing. Everything seemed to be rising up. Suddenly they saw that the big bay window was bowing in. It was bowing in two or three inches, all the way across the front of the room. Roscoe pressed his hands flat against it to stop it and, feeling the incredible pressure, he began trembling all over. He could barely speak. "Mike, you're right. This is Hugo."

They were pushing on the glass together, but the window was like rubber. It kept bowing above and below their hands, making a grinding, straining sound as if it were going to burst. It was beginning to leak around the edges. The water had risen even higher and Roscoe knew it was at least six or eight feet high under the house. And it was still rising.

"Shit, Mike. The whole ocean's coming at us."

Mike kept pushing. "If we have to go, I'm saying *if*, what do we do if we get separated?

"Dammit, we hold on to each other's belts or something. We ain't getting separated." Mike nodded and kept on pushing. "Yeah, but let's just say we do. Let's make a plan."

Roscoe joked halfheartedly. "You grab the first whale and I'll grab Flipper. Push, Mike! Push hard."

The window bulged in on them and they pushed as hard as they could. Mike was still pushing when he heard Buckles growling. He turned and squinted. "Oh my God!"

Roscoe said, "What?"

"The kitchen!"

The linoleum that covered the kitchen floor was bubbling up in the center. It was pulsing and rising up, as if it were a giant balloon getting ready to pop. Mike screamed, "What the fuck is that?"

"Beats the hell out of me. Push, man! Push!"

9 ≶

Bracing for the Strike

In the months following Hugo, the Strom Thurmond Institute of Government and Public Affairs analyzed the effectiveness with which regional emergency plans had dealt with widespread disruption of services. They found that forecasts of hurricane-force winds and storm surges were primarily centered on the coastal areas, which led to the conclusion by officials bracing for the strike that the coastal areas would be the hardest hit and would require the greatest emergency response preparation. By the time it was discovered that inland cities such as Sumter, Camden, Lancaster, and even Charlotte, North Carolina, had been hit almost as hard, the emergency crews and facilities had already located their operations along the coast and had to redeploy. The Institute recommended that in the future the emergency planners prepare for the worst, not just the expected. This would make sure that no part of the state would be without help if, like Hugo, the disaster was more extensive than past experience had led planners to expect.

Another finding of the Institute, which was working with the help of the National Association of State Energy Officials and the U.S. Department of Energy, was that few states, counties, or communities in the United States have enough emergency generators, technical personnel, and other equipment to cope independently with a natural disaster the size and the scope of a storm such as Hugo.

The energy industry has historically developed and maintained emergency energy plans, and Hugo illustrated quite clearly how critical such preemergency planning was in getting the energy infrastructure restored. Even so, utility preparations can only go so far. Government has to step in, and the Institute's report showed that in the case of Hugo, government was not always up to the task. While states already have emergency response organizations (usually the State Adjutant General or the Emergency Preparedness Division), the Thurmond Institute noted that dealing with severe energy response and recovery operations requires a level of technical, legal, and economic expertise that does not normally exist in most state organizations. For all the preparation, Hurricane Hugo threw South Carolina into a state of confusion.

Electricity was a common denominator: losing it meant severe problems, getting it back caused more problems, but having it back was essential for solving other problems. Some emergency generators, both private and public, were in place when Hugo hit, and helped speed the recovery. But they presented problems of their own, the Institute noted:

> Generators ranging from large capacity models to small house-sized units proved invaluable during Hurricane Hugo in maintaining health, safety and security. Portable sources of power during an emergency of this kind are particularly important to those retail establishments in rural communities that must provide milk, ice, food, gasoline and other such goods during recovery. Portable emergency generators are also essential for life support equipment in the home and on dairy and poultry farms. However, the public must be educated on the proper operation of these small, portable generators so as to prevent property damage and serious personal injuries that can be caused by inadequately energizing the larger electric power system.

Even though the number of casualties *during* Hurricane Hugo was lower than during previous hurricanes due to better forecasting, evacuation, and preparation, many lives were lost *after* the storm during the restoration period due to accidents such as electrocution, fires, stress-related heart attacks, and tree-clearing mishaps. The Institute reported that

half of the post-storm fatalities were energy-related, resulting from house fires caused by using candles for light, and electrocution from downed wires and portable generators. The most serious electric safety accidents involved backfeeding current from portable generators into downed lines, injuring numerous repair crewmen and killing at least four.

Portable generators would be plugged into household systems but the operator would forget, or wouldn't know, that the power generated would feed back out into downed lines, leaving live wires dangerously exposed. This could have been eliminated by the operator simply disconnecting the meter or shutting off the circuit breaker. Just before the storm, and when it became apparent which areas would be damaged by it, the utilities withdrew their other ads from radio and television and substituted safety ads in their place. South Carolina Electric & Gas ran a radio and television announcement over and over again in the aftermath of the storm warning of live wires, but in many areas there was no radio or television, so no one was listening.

In most cases, communications were lost as soon as the major force of the storm hit. Those commercial phone circuits that remained in service were quickly overtaxed by public use. The Emergency Broadcast System was lost hours before the brunt of the storm. Particularly efficient before and after the storm were cellular telephones (used extensively by the utility companies and government personnel) and the South Carolina Law Enforcement Division statewide FM radio network with its automatic repeaters. Fax machines allowed utilities to exchange technical material and work together more effectively.

Right after the storm swept through, the National Guard flew helicopter missions to assess damage, perform search and rescue missions, and ferry work crews and officials to the barrier islands and outlying areas. They also directed traffic, assisted with the cleanup effort, installed portable generators to get the power back on for lighting, pumped water, and got sewage facilities operating again.

Two days before the storm hit, the governor had authorized the Guard to activate units along the coast and throughout the state, and to take preparatory actions such as preloading heavy equipment (bulldozers and front-end loaders) on transporters, perform operational checks of communications units, check fuel storage and handling, and deploy electric generators. The Guard had 214 generators varying in capacity from 1.5 kilowatts to 100 kilowatts and, counting equipment borrowed from other states, the total number of generators available—with trained operators—was 250.

National Guard units were the main crews that were to clear the trees and keep the roads free of large debris. This enabled line crews from the utilities to restore electric service in many areas. When required, the Guard also performed crowd control. Some electrical power officials felt that there could have been a closer working relationship between the military and the utilities. For example, some military units cleared rights-of-way for transmission lines without coordinating with the utilities. In some instances, military crews cleared trees and debris from the roads and placed them in the rights-of-way of power lines, thus hampering, and in some cases even preventing, repair crews from reaching downed transmission lines.

The Thurmond Institute concludes:

> The main lesson learned from Hurricane Hugo is that it is possible for government and industry to work together efficiently and effectively to mitigate the effects of such a massive natural disaster. . . . However, there should be continuing review of this experience and the lessons learned from it in

order to improve coordination between and among federal, state, and local government agencies and the energy industry in planning for and coping with disasters of this type and magnitude.

While all this is wonderfully true, the odd thing is that nowhere in this exhaustive report is there one mention of simply burying electrical lines to save lives in the future. Not only do electric line configurations ruin a town's skyline—in the poorer sections they seem to have been strung by lunatics—during a hurricane everything about them—the poles, the lines, and the insulators—can be absolutely lethal. After the storm, generator feedback can make downed lines lethal again. This problem was not mentioned. No solution—except urging crewmen to be more careful—was even suggested in the report.

Horace was still asleep on the swing when Rambo and Molly woke him around seven-thirty. They were on the porch and both were pacing up and down. Molly was making little yipping sounds and whining and Rambo was growling. The chickens were up under the porch, and from the noise they were making, he thought something was after them. Then he saw Joe running toward him, waving his arms and yelling, "Hugo's back! It's heading right for us!"

Horace stood up and matter-of-factly said, "I've got to get these windows." But his pulse began thumping in his ears.

Joe agreed. "Give me a hammer and I'll help. Mine are all set."

While they were pounding in the nails they listened to a Savannah station on the console radio in the living room. The announcer was saying that the prediction was for a twenty-foot tidal surge and it was sounding as if McClellanville was right in the center of it. Horace groaned. "Damn, that's going to kill the boats."

The wind was definitely up and a high whistling sound was in the air. Both dogs were pacing faster and now they were baying. Horace spat and shook his head. "That's exactly what I didn't want to hear. Dogs know when these things are coming."

After they finished the windows they rolled the rugs and, using pliers to twist coat hanger wire, they tied them tight and stacked them up on the dressers. Then, taking the food from the lower shelves and the clothes from the lower drawers, they loaded it in plastic bags and hung them from nails they'd driven in the wall up near the ceiling. After pounding out all of the Sheetrock panels in the bedroom ceiling, they began wrestling the rugs, the clothes, and the mattresses up and onto the ceiling beams in the attic. It was hard and painful work and Horace couldn't help cursing. "That sonofabitch who took the handles off mattresses ought to have his balls cut off."

Joe was below him, straining under the big queen-size. "It's like lifting a fat drunk."

When they had stored everything they could up in the attic, and everything else as high as they could get it, they opened two more beers, finished them, and headed for their boats. Both Horace and Joe had played football and run track back at McClellanville High School, and they were both in good shape. They jogged down the dirt road, Molly and Rambo running alongside, all the way down to the dock.

The boats had already been tied off with double and triple lines and lashed to the twelve-foot-high pilings in front of the fish house. Every anchor they could find was in use and they had even rigged up two ancient coal stoves, which weighed at least two hundred pounds each, and chained them to the sterns and dropped them in too. The shrimp nets had been folded and stowed away, and every porthole and opening had been closed and battened down. As they checked the boats over they realized that they should have made a try to get out of there that morning. Joe yelled out, "We should have made a run for it up the river."

Horace agreed, but now it was too late. "You're right about that."

Then he slapped Joe on the back. "Hell, it'll never get back here. We're too far back. Come on, let's see how Salter's doing."

Captain Stanley Salter, the owner of the sixty-eight-foot shrimper *Mermaid,* had made three decisions that morning for himself and his crew of three: LeRoy Nealy, David Balou, and Jerry Pittman. One, he would not go to Jacksonville or Wilmington or up the Wando or the Waccamaw rivers. Two, he would not tie his boat up to the pier the way everyone else was doing, including Horace and Joe. And three, he was bound and determined to ride this hurricane out or die trying.

As Horace and Joe climbed on board the *Mermaid,* Stan Salter came out of the cabin, shouting above the wind and the heavy engine noise. "Hey, boys, nice day for a little boat ride!"

Horace hollered, "We just wanted to see how crazy you were! You really going to do it?"

"Well, I'm going to damn sure try."

Salter had lined the *Mermaid*'s sides with automobile tires to keep the damage down, and double-tied the boat to a big two-hundred-foot steel barge anchored at the pier. His engine was on and the diesel smoke was streaming out over the deck. He cupped his hand over his mouth and shouted, "Nothing is lifting this much weight. If it takes us, it's got to take the barge."

Horace shook his head. "But what if it does?"

Salter studied him a moment as the wind dropped. "In that case, my ass is grass and I'm probably going to be lining up for food stamps. But I'll be damned if I'm going up the river and just sit there like a duck." He grinned and popped his hands together. "Come on along. I got plenty room and plenty beer."

He called out to his first mate, LeRoy Nealy, who was below deck in the galley. LeRoy stuck his head up and Salter yelled, asking him what was for dinner. LeRoy yelled back, "Stew and we got some tomatoes and rice. Those boys coming along?"

Salter yelled, "Y'all want to change your mind? LeRoy says he's serving beef stew."

Horace grinned. "Is it any good?"

Salter shrugged. "Let's say it's interesting."

Horace shook his head. "Sorry, Stan, it would be fun but I've got kids. You know how it is."

The wind was picking up again and Salter had to yell even louder. "Ahh, I'm just kidding. That stew will kill you quicker than any damn hurricane. Good luck, now."

Horace yelled, "You're the one that's going to need the luck! How far you think it's out?"

Suddenly the wind surged—stronger, much stronger—and in the dusk Horace could see the tin roof on the fish house beginning to flutter. The big SLOW, NO WAKE sign out in the channel was spinning and looked like it would go any minute.

Horace shouted again, "How far you think it's out?"

Captain Salter looked at the darkness out over the marsh, the bay, and the ocean. He called to LeRoy, "You better start serving! This thing's closing fast." Then he shouted at Horace. "Ten minutes, maybe twenty. You better be going! I've got work to do!" Joe and Horace hopped onto the deck but lingered there, watching the rising storm.

Stan Salter had made two serious miscalculations. One was that he didn't need to go on to Jacksonville that morning. And two, that he would have time to swing the *Mermaid*'s bow into the wind and then tie it to the barge. Now the wind was too strong and the stern was facing the wind and there wasn't time to do anything but do what he was doing, and that was to keep the engine in reverse.

Adjusting the wheel so he could tie it off, Salter checked the cabin to make sure everything was set. The boat's stern was directly into the wind, and the engine was on full reverse to hold it there. The *Mermaid* had three big lights for working the shrimp and Salter had them all on.

As the smoke from the *Mermaid*'s engine whipped back in Horace's face, he could see it sweeping up over the fish house and into the big oaks that ringed the tiny village. He could feel and hear the wind seemingly changing gears. It was charging the air with so much electricity that the hair on the back of his neck and the backs of his hands was standing straight up and quivering. He'd never seen that before. Above, the clouds looked black and purple and the sky all around was a phosphorescent green. With the three shafts of light from the *Mermaid* crisscrossing in the blowing spray, he saw something that at first he refused to believe. Then he yelled and pointed. "Joe! Look!"

The lights were creating a stroboscopic effect in the clouds; it was a sight he knew he would never forget.

One evening, years ago, just before sundown, Horace had pulled into Charleston Harbor and he'd seen the church steeples of St. Michael's and St. John's, and the three blocks of houses that loop around the Battery, all reflected in a pink and rose cloud cover. It was Charleston reflected upside down in a fiery light that was so beautiful he felt like crying. Later, all he had to do, at almost any time, was close his eyes and he could see it still. But now he was looking at something at the other end of the spectrum. Something altogether different; something absolutely terrifying. The dark and rushing clouds under Captain Stan Salter's lights were revealing the very face of the hurricane and it was rising up before them like a giant cliff—black, monstrous, absolutely evil, absolutely unstoppable. The lights were defining it as it was coming off the ocean, as it was crossing the marsh and the bay, and as it headed up tiny Jeremy Creek toward them, toward McClellanville. In a few minutes it would be on them.

Horace couldn't believe he was actually seeing the front end of the hurricane, actually about to be overwhelmed by it. He grabbed Joe's shoulder. "You see what I see?"

Joe nodded. "I'm afraid so."

The pressure was incredible and their ears popped and rang. The wind went higher, shriller, louder, and all around them everything was suddenly coming apart. The tin roofs of the fish house buildings were peeling back and they could feel the pier beneath them beginning to vibrate. Then, without saying another word, they grinned at each other. They got down in the sprint position, with their right knees and both hands on the ground.

Horace grinned and yelled, "Just like against Edisto!"

Joe laughed. "Let's give them hell!"

Captain Salter was frantically waving both hands at them from his cabin, telling them to run for it. The waves were higher, the foam was washing up into the cabin, and even the ground was shaking. But still Horace and Joe waited. And waited. Horace shouted, "Almost!"

Neither of them spoke, they didn't have to. They waited, because now they were in another grip. Something elemental and primal had cut in that they hadn't felt since high school. It was something that they'd never be able to explain, but it was something like being in the huddle with the game on the line. One of those crazy moments when there was no tomorrow, where a mistake, any mistake, would mean that it was all over.

Suddenly the long dock started to ripple beneath them. The boards began popping loose and the boats moored to it were bouncing wildly. Captain Salter's lights were pinpointed on the boats and he was blowing his horn. Horace said only one word, "Now!" and they tore across the shipyard and back up the Mc-Clellanville Road faster than they'd ever run in their lives, with the dogs howling at their heels. The full force of the hurricane had hit them and all they could do was run or be caught up in it. Pieces of gravel, clam shells, and tin cans hit them and big planks from the pier whirled by, making thrumming, boomerang sounds. But they kept their heads down and kept streaking. Directly in front, a huge pine tree thundered across the road with so much force it shook the ground. Molly stopped and shrieked louder than before. Off to the other side, an enormous oak came crashing down; its root system blocked out everything and was dropping clods of dirt as big as sofas; a tin roof from one of the dock shacks sailed by, sounding like a guillotine.

They raced across Horace's backyard and made it to the door with the storm pounding them right into the steps. Inside, they dropped exhausted to the floor, unable to move, unable to speak. Horace held his head in between his legs, waiting for his breath to come back. The house was shaking as if God had picked it up and was going to tip it upside down and shake them out. The wind streamed under it and over it and both of them felt it lifting and then settling and then lifting again.

Horace's first thought was his kids; the second, his roof. The kids were safe in the brand-new brick Lincoln High School, but if one shingle of his roof peeled off, it would start a chain reaction that wouldn't stop until every one was gone.

He yelled, "Joe, I'm going out to check the shingles!"

Joe didn't even look over. "You do, and you're going alone. You can't see shit."

"I can see enough."

Horace filled his pockets with roofing nails and, with a hammer in each pocket, in case one fell out, he opened the front door. The wind was howling, but he was on the lee side and for a moment he thought there would be no trouble. Keeping close to the wall, he began easing himself around the corner. His right arm and shoulder first, then his right leg. The pressure of the wind was incredible, his ears felt as if they were going to explode, but he kept close to the wall and close to the floor. He took another sliding step, then another. Suddenly, he was picked up and slung flat on his back. He flailed out to grab something, anything, and grabbed a porch post. He clung to it, trying to catch his breath, trying to get a better grip. Desperately he wrapped his arms around it and held on as he felt the full blast on his legs and heard his shirt and pants flapping so fast they sounded like a bad tire coming apart. One shoe came off. Slowly, and keeping as low to the floor as he could, he worked his way back toward the door.

He'd forgotten to tie the swing down and it was banging on the ceiling, falling apart. As he inched down the porch, clinging to the posts, he heard his dogs whining. They were out of the wind, but they were trapped under the porch stairs. They'd seen him and they came sliding up the steps on their bellies. He reached down and grabbed Molly by the back of her neck and levered her up with him. Then he pulled Rambo up by his front leg.

Slowly he crawled across the porch and, with one hand on each dog, he made it back to the door. As he forced it open and held it for the dogs, he heard the beer cans trapped in the corner of the porch. They were bouncing and ricocheting on the spokes so fast they sounded like a stick being dragged along a picket fence.

He bolted the door behind him. "Damn, it knocked me flat on my ass."

Joe was on the phone. He had located the twins, Tonya and Wanda, and he handed the phone to Horace. They both came on talking at once, which was fine with him, because he needed to find another pair of shoes and he wanted to catch his breath. Someone had told them the hurricane was called Margo and they wanted Horace to settle it. Horace smiled as he told them it was Hugo. "Are you getting plenty to eat up there?"

They said they'd had hot dogs and Pepsi-Colas and later they were going to have ice cream.

"Okay," Horace said. "Let's hang up now. There's a lot of people there that want to call out. I'll be up in a little while. Okay?"

"Okay, Daddy."

"And don't forget, I love you. And if your momma calls, tell her I love her, too."

"Okay, Daddy. We love you too, Daddy."

Horace hung up and looked out desperately toward Lincoln High School. Somehow he had to get to his girls. Everything was dark, but when a transformer blew he saw that the big oak that had fallen was *his* big oak, and its root system was higher than his roof. In the blinding light he saw that a tin roof had wrapped itself around one of the porch posts and was flapping. Shingles, glass, chickenwire and hogwire fencing were flying through the air and raining on the porch along with rocks, oyster shells, clam shells, hunks of coral, and sheets of screen. The chickens were squawking hysterically, and down the porch under the disintegrating swing he saw a flounder, as wide as a license plate, gasping for breath and flapping.

"Jesus," Horace said. "We've got to get to the school. This thing's getting worse."

Joe was looking around frantically for his flashlight. "How about the dogs?"

"The hell with them. They've got food. I've got kids to worry about."

10 〜

Rough Edges

Dead center between Charleston and Myrtle Beach lies the 250,000-acre Francis Marion National Forest. It is one of the few national forests with a salt marsh within its boundaries, and thus claims some of the most diverse wildlife and habitat in the United States. Before Hugo this preserve was considered a jewel of a forest for its stands of longleaf pine, oak, cypress, and hickory. But it was more than a jewel to the red-cockaded woodpecker, a bird that can live only in mature longleaf pines fourteen inches wide and at least fifty years old. The bird nests only in cavities which are formed when mature trees drop limbs. Francis Marion provided this ideal habitat in abundance. When Hugo struck, it killed an estimated 60 percent of the endangered woodpecker population. Under the onslaught of 140- to 200-mph winds, nesting trees snapped off just at the cavity, where the trunk was weakest, and the birds were flung out into the night.

One of the great publicity hustles in South Carolina is the paper mills assuring the public that the word *harvest,* which is normally used for crops like corn or wheat or collards, also applies to trees. Indeed, some of the paper mill advertising informs us that the mills carefully and scientifically replant the trees in such a manner that the animals and birds and aquatic life live on virtually undisturbed. From this we might assume that the red-cockaded could simply fly over a few miles to the commercially owned paper mill forest, set up housekeeping, and live happily ever after.

What the mills don't say is that the fast-growing loblolly

pines they "harvest" every fifteen or twenty years have the singular quality of being able to support virtually no animal or bird life. The loblolly, while it has a wonderfully Southern-sounding name—it actually *sounds* like an ideal habitat for squirrels, possum, raccoons—grows no nuts or berries; it produces nothing but shade and cheap timber. A squirrel, a possum, or a raccoon would starve if it had to count on a loblolly forest. The red-cockaded woodpecker would find no shelter there.

The damage to forests and wildlife habitats done by Hurricane Hugo on the night of September 22, 1989, will last for lifetimes. Governor Carroll Campbell, after looking at the beaches, said, "You go down these beaches, and there is no beach. It's gone. It will come back, but it will be different. . . . We don't know what to rebuild. We may rebuild, and we may retreat, because we've lost so much."

Beaches may come back to something resembling what they once were, but not even the very young today will live long enough to see the Francis Marion Forest the way it was before the storm. Eventually, given time, it will come back, but many are not waiting for time alone to solve the problems. Already the U.S. Forest Service has been quick to create artificial cavities for the red-cockaded woodpeckers. Holes are routed out of older pines similar to the ones the woodpeckers would make. And, just as the birds do, the workers punch resin wells through the bark below and around the cavities to produce the sticky drip of pine sap that discourages tree-climbing snakes and other predators from coming into the nest.

The most recent report from the Forest Service is that a few of the red-cockaded woodpeckers have accepted the artificial cavities and are reproducing. But the woodpecker is competing for space: eleven other kinds of birds, five mammals, and bees have also made use of this shelter.

George Garris, the refuge manager of Cape Romain, said he

believes that succession in the maritime forest has been set back a hundred years or more on some of the barrier islands, especially Bull Island. But Garris, in an interview with *South Carolina Wildlife,* tried to talk about what survived, rather than what was lost. "We found five turkey hens and three toms right after the storm. And the red wolves are in excellent shape," he said, adding that there were four wolf pups found residing on Bull Island. "While there are few marsh rabbits, the red wolf's favorite food, there are plenty of raccoons and other prey available. The remarkable thing is that these wolves were still pups when Hugo hit, born in May '89 on Mother's Day." Also in good shape, at least at this time, are the three endangered species of turtle—the green sea turtle, the leatherback, and the hawkbill.

Small game biologist Breck Carmichael said, "Although our squirrels will readily build leaf nests in trees, they prefer hollows, and those den-tree nesting places are gone. Their long-term problem is that they are so dependent upon nuts from trees for food, particularly oaks. Those will take fifty years to come back, so we are looking at a long time for squirrel habitat to recover."

Dr. Gene Wood, professor of forest wildlife ecology at Clemson University, also in an interview with *South Carolina Wildlife,* said that Hugo surged over the barrier islands all the way from Folly Island to Huntington Beach and left them vulnerable to erosion. In some places the primary dune and interdune areas were flattened. These zones are the nesting habitat for sea turtles and shore birds, he said, and it will be years before they recover. Wood added that of the 700 to 800 fox squirrels on Bull Island, once the densest population in the world, only half remained. The survivors will have a difficult time finding food. These squirrels are much larger than gray squirrels, with black fur, a long, bushy tail, a white nose, and white ears. Wood thinks that it may be impossible for the fox

squirrel population to recover to its old strength in fewer than
sixty to seventy years. But, he said, they too will return—
given time.

Two years after Hugo, the U.S. Forest Service embarked on
a plan to restore the 250,000 acres that were so severely damaged in Francis Marion. About 2.5 million trees, most of them
longleaf pine, have since been planted. Another 1.3 million
were to be planted in 1991. But the new Forest Service plan—
the details of which were still being negotiated late in 1991—
is even more ambitious. Never before has such a large-scale
replanting and restoration been attempted. The new plan will
spell out the remaining tree varieties to be planted, the number of new trees to be harvested, and how the forest will be
managed. The timber interests, of course, will want the Forest
Service to replant and replenish the commercially valuable
loblolly pine, and "manage" the forest carefully.

Richard Shelter of the Forest Service, in an interview with
The State, said that if intensive "management" is continued,
complete with herbicides and land preparation, loblolly pines
will be "as thick as dog hairs." And Pete Kirby, a forest expert
for the Wildlife Society, added, "the Forest Service for decades
has been devoted to logging fast and furious. This is the chance
to change."

The State continued,

> While Francis Marion is the second largest watershed on
> the East Coast and one of the most ecologically diverse areas
> in the world, more than 25,000 acres of it is in private hands.
>
> Glen A. Stapleton, who, as district ranger, is responsible
> for management and care of the forest along with the envi-
> ronmentalists, views the Francis Marion debate as the first
> major test of the Forest Service's approach. And while all
> sides concede that relations so far have been very open, envi-
> ronmental groups remain wary.
>
> Dana Beach, executive director of the South Carolina

Coastal Conservation League, said, "We aren't going to be naive enough to think just because the Forest Service is saying the right thing it will do the right thing. Clear cutting and logging here continue at a pace greater than what is taking place in Brazil and Malaysia."

And Jane Lareau, a member of the South Carolina Coastal Conservation League, said, "We want the Forest Service to stop pushing the forest to its limits for maximum timber production."

We will soon know the details of the plan and in 1992 we will see it in action, but it will take much more than this to restore the Francis Marion. It will take years.

Time, of course, will soften the rough edges of the landscape that were scraped away by Hugo. It will help the eagle re-thatch her nest and show the osprey where to build out of the reach of the paper mill forests. The longleaf pine nesting habitat will eventually come back for the red-cockaded woodpecker, the oaks will start dropping acorns and nuts will fall from the hickory, the pecan, and the walnut. And there will be a shady cover for the wild turkey and a clearing where the red fox can slip through the forest to stalk and catch its prey. All this will take time but eventually it will come.

―――――

It was into the front edge of the storm that Horace and Joe drove on their way to Lincoln High School in the pickup truck with the dogs. Horace had planned to leave them at home, but when he'd tried to close the door on them they wouldn't get out of the way. They knew they were going to be left behind, and were so determined to go that he had finally caved in and let them hop in the front of the truck where they crouched on the floor. When they left the house it was almost nine-thirty and it was pitch dark.

The high school was the designated evacuation center for the area. Most of McClellanville had been there since morning. Teenagers and young adults had been assembled in the big cafeteria, which had a raised stage at one end for school plays and speeches. The older people, and the small children and infants, were in the home economics room and the classrooms.

Horace quickly thanked God he'd brought Rambo and Molly along, because even in the crowd of over 1,100 it took the dogs only a few minutes to find the twins. They were in a group in one of the classrooms off the main hallway. Tonya and Wanda flung themselves into his arms and clung so tight he had to pry them loose. "Easy now. Easy now. You get in touch with your momma?"

"Yeah, Daddy," Wanda said. "She's really worried about you."

"Yeah, but she'll be okay," Tonya added.

Horace hugged them both again. "Boy, it's good to see you two. Everything's going to be all right now."

For the next two hours, until 1 A.M., while the front end of Hugo raged outside and the tall pines thundered to the ground, Horace and Joe, the two children, and the dogs sat together in a classroom with thirty-two other people. Outside, pine trees 100 and 150 feet high were slamming into the ground with so much force the entire building shook. Joe said it was a good thing it wasn't daytime because people would have panicked and run outside and been killed by the trees and the flying rocks.

In the cafeteria, the teachers and group leaders were making the small kids play word games and sing songs. The teenagers would have none of that, and most of them stayed off to the side with Walkmans glued to their ears, listening to the latest music. The adults helped serve coffee and sandwiches, which Jennings Austin, the principal, had provided. After that, they sat down at the cafeteria tables and began playing cards.

All during the front part of the hurricane no one really thought there would be any serious danger. The building was almost brand new and the walls were brick with steel supports. As a matter of fact, the building was so well insulated that the sound of the big trees falling was muffled and the howling wind was reduced to a whisper. In the small classrooms many of the adults who didn't want to play board games, or gossip, put two chairs together and put their feet up and went to sleep. By one-thirty even Horace was beginning to get bored.

But somewhere around one-forty in the morning Horace felt something happening. Something was changing. It took a few minutes before he realized that the eye of the storm had arrived and was passing over. The winds had stopped; it was dead still. He went to the window and saw a strange, almost sickly, phosphorescent light in the sky. McClellanville had lost all of its power when the storm hit; now it was being illuminated by the lightning and the pulsing green sky. In the dark hall behind him a door opened and someone shouted that it was over. Then some of the kids started down the hall, toward the front door. Backlit by the tiny auxiliary lights up on the ceiling, Horace could see a string of people leaving the building. He shouted, "Hey, stop! Don't go out there! Stop!"

But they were too far away to hear him; they were already outside. Then a sheriff's deputy came rushing down the hall bellowing over a bullhorn. He had a big, deep voice, and when he shouted for quiet, he got it. "All right! Now everybody just get back on in here. You heard me. Back in. This thing's only half over. The worst is coming. You go out there now and you'll get yourself killed. And somebody lock that damn door!"

Slowly the crowd came shuffling back in, single file, solemnly following one another up the long hall and taking their seats on the cafeteria floor and in the classrooms.

Horace and Joe and the kids sat in the same place they'd been sitting, in the classroom seats. Together, with the others, they managed to look like they were waiting for a teacher to call the roll for the class to start. On the blackboard were the lessons in American History; one wall was covered with the battles of the Civil War.

Suddenly the dogs, who were being petted by the smaller kids, shook them off and began a high, piercing whine. Horace went to the window to listen and watch, but all that was there was the green and eerie stillness. The dogs were getting more and more frantic. Horace knew it had to be a tornado.

Neither Horace nor Joe, nor for that matter anyone in the school, had the faintest idea that directly behind the wall of the hurricane's eye an avalanche of water twenty to twenty-five feet high was looming up, getting ready to roll down on Lincoln High School. They'd heard there would be a tidal surge, possibly a big one, but nothing could have prepared them for what was about to happen.

Horace kept looking out into the eye. The light was greener and clearer now, and he could see that the tiny leaves at the tops of the trees were motionless and the Spanish moss was hanging straight down. The temperature had risen at least twenty degrees and the humidity had dropped with it. Nothing was stirring in the hot vacuum. He felt the hair on the back of his hands stand up and his skin start itching, and he realized how nervous and tense he'd suddenly become. Still, there was no sound, no movement. But he knew something was out there, something terrible, and it was scaring him. He squatted down, picked his girls up in his arms and, trying not to let them know he was scared, he held them tight.

For a few more minutes it was dead quiet. Nothing. Then out of the darkness, out of that nothing, came the big, black, silent wave crashing into the school. The wave slammed into the east side of the building with so much force it pushed the air conditioning and heater units right out of their casements. At first the noise was low and muted and was felt more than it was heard, but the building shook as if an earthquake had struck. Without any warning, and with very little sound, a solid foot of water came cascading down the halls and into the rooms. Someone screamed, "We're being flooded! My God, look at it!"

The foot of water was suddenly a foot and a half and then two feet, and everyone was screaming and holding on to one another and anything they could grab. Plaster began falling, dishes clattered in the kitchen, and tables and desks were tossed around like toys. The water pressure was so strong it was knocking down interior walls like dominoes.

Someone shouted, "Where's it coming from?"

And someone else screamed, "We're going to drown like rats! We're trapped! Why'd they put us here!"

The cries of "Mama, Mama! Daddy, Daddy!" rose from the trapped and petrified children. Horace held his daughters close. Tonya was crying for Olly May, and Wanda was squeezing his neck tight. Joe lifted the dogs up on a work table and held them together. The other parents began standing their kids up on the desks and tables and holding them up on their shoulders. It was panic, pure panic. People were screaming, shouting, pleading, praying. The building shook again and again with the pounding of another wave and then another. Everyone was sure it would collapse any minute. It was just a matter of time before they would be flushed out into the raging waters and thundering trees.

Horace held his kids tight, determined not to turn them loose for a second. A high, thin voice, which sounded no older than three, rang out, "I want my mama! I want my mama!"

Horace freed a hand and cut on his flashlight. He could taste the saltwater on his lips as he checked the level on the bottom slat of the window. It was now three feet high and rising fast. The outside walls were holding, but he didn't know for how long. If they could keep above the water they had a chance; if they couldn't, they would simply drown.

Everyone in the classroom seemed to be screaming as the water kept rising and the desks began floating. They didn't know where to go or what to do, and the only light came from a single flashlight and the tiny auxiliary lights out in the hall. It was impossible for anyone to take charge. It was bedlam and every second the water kept rising. The adults couldn't do anything but hold the kids higher and keep them from getting wet for a few more minutes.

Horace, standing in water above his waist, had Tonya hooked on to his left hip and Wanda on his right. Wanda cupped her hand over his ear and told him she had to go to the bathroom. He turned and whispered that it was all right to go right there, just don't tell anybody. She cried, "Daddy!"

Horace, with the kids in his arms, looked around and saw that all of the men and women were holding kids up as high as they could hold them. Even though he was now standing on a desk two and a half feet high, the water was above his knees and he knew it wouldn't stop until it filled the room. Something had to happen soon or everyone would be jammed against the ceiling trying to breathe and then, if the water kept coming, they would all drown.

He knew he had to do something, and quickly. He handed the kids to Joe and, standing on a desk, he reached up and tapped on the Sheetrock ceiling panel with his flashlight. It wasn't plastered in or nailed in, and when he pushed against it, it lifted right up. He slid the panel to one side, out of the way, then he moved another one. He wanted to shove the kids up where they would be out of the water, where they could breathe. But first he had to know if the supporting rails were thick enough and strong enough to support them.

Hooking his fingers over the rail he pulled down. It gave easily and almost broke. It would never hold much weight by itself, so he began crisscrossing the panels over the rails for more support. Taking Wanda from Joe, he raised her over his head and carefully eased her up onto the ceiling crawl. "Darling, I want you to lay down. Now you've got to do it right and you can't move. Understand?"

"Yes, Daddy."

He kept coaching her as he slid her carefully onto the panels where she stretched out as if she were standing at attention with her arms down at her sides. "Like this?"

"That's it, darling. Perfect. Now just stay right there and I'm going to make Tonya do exactly like you."

"But how about Rambo?"

"He'll be fine."

After Tonya was in place, Horace said, "Now listen. We're putting a couple more kids up there with you. There's plenty of room so lie real close, like hot dogs."

After giving each new kid careful instructions about what to do in the dark crawlspace, and holding them fast until they were positioned, he slid three more up onto the panels. As he lifted them up, one after the other, he realized that he was doing the only thing he could do. If he could just keep his kids and a few more from drowning, that would be all anyone could do.

The other adults had seen what Horace had worked out with the ceiling panels and they began doing the same. But the water kept coming and the tables and desks they were standing on were afloat, tipping and shifting. Horace kept track of the water by watching the slat in the window. It was now at five feet. If it continued, the adults would drown first; there was no escape. If they climbed up with the kids, the rails would collapse. If they stood on the desks and the tables and the water kept rising, they would drown. Everyone was trapped. No one could get out of the room, and if the water didn't stop, they were all dead.

He checked the window slat again and groaned. The water was still rising. Tonya hollered down, "Daddy, how's Rambo and Molly?"

Horace looked over and saw Molly. He didn't see Rambo.

"They're fine. Guess how they're swimming?"

"How?" Tonya said.

Horace grinned up at them. "They're dog-paddling."

"Daddy!" Wanda laughed and the other kids joined in.

Horace said, "Quit moving around, y'all. Remember, make like hot dogs."

He smiled for a second. Then he checked the window slat and felt the blood drain from his face. The water was up another four inches and was now almost six feet deep. He knew if it kept rising it would soon be all over. In another minute or so he would tell Tonya and Wanda that when it got to them they would have to balance themselves carefully on the thin panels and stretch up and up, and try to breathe the air up close to the roof. He would also have to tell them to keep looking up and not look down. What he wasn't telling them was that he didn't want them seeing what was going to happen to him and Joe.

11 ⇒

The Damage

It is estimated that property damage caused by Hurricane Hugo exceeded $6 billion in South Carolina alone. Another $400 million in damage was caused in North Carolina and an estimated $2 billion in the Caribbean. Twenty-four of South Carolina's 46 counties and 29 of North Carolina's 100 counties were declared disaster areas in the aftermath. Eighty-two people died; twelve in Puerto Rico, six in the U.S. Virgin Islands, twenty-three elsewhere in the Caribbean, and forty-one on the U.S. mainland. Thirty-five deaths in South Carolina and North Carolina were attributed to Hugo; surprisingly, only fifteen of these occurred during the passage of the storm. Figures indicated that human casualties during this hurricane were fewer than during previous storms due to better forecasting, evacuation, and preparation. Most deaths occurred after the storm.

With the evacuation came a series of problems so serious and so demanding that they could have proved overwhelming. More than 150,000 people had to be evacuated from the coastal region and, since no one knew exactly where they would be safe, many headed for inland towns like Sumter and Camden and Charlotte only to find that they were still in the storm's path. The traffic on Interstate 26 and Interstate 20 heading away from the coast was so heavy that a normal two-hour drive from Charleston to Columbia or from Myrtle Beach to Columbia was seven or eight hours despite the fact that all four lanes had been designated outbound. The drivers and their families, not knowing where to go, kept heading inland and kept trying to get a motel for the night. They soon realized that they were trying to do what another 150,000 evacuees were trying to do. The motel rooms had all been rented and there was nothing else to do but keep on driving and keep on looking. Out on the road the cars were bumper-to-bumper, every phone had a long line waiting, and every gas station was backed up twenty and thirty cars deep. For those families lucky enough to find a room for the night, the luck soon swung the other way. The storm took out all of the power, and without power there was no light, no pumps for the gas, no refrigeration, and in many cases no water. Many of the families who spent that terrible night huddled together in a motel room, the storm blasting away at the windows and flooding the hallways, said they would have been much better off if they had just kept on driving and never stopped until late the next day.

Power was out for weeks after the storm in some communities. The following list of electrical utility customers out of service is an indication of the monumental work that went into rebuilding the system:

Utility	Customers Affected	Total Customers
S.C. Electric & Gas	300,000	427,000
Carolina Power & Light	140,000	931,000
Duke Power	697,000	1,565,000
Electrical Cooperatives	300,000	409,000
S.C. Public Service Authority	85,899	85,902

These figures may be misleading because they do not reflect the amount of work that went into getting just one customer back on line. The case of McClellanville would be a better example of just what went into restoration. SCE&G brought in a generator as quickly as possible to meet the municipal needs, but the transmission lines to the town had been devastated. Thirty-nine H-frame poles were down and another seventy were badly leaning. Crews having to work in this swampy terrain soon discovered they were working in deep mud and water up to their waists. Large mats had to be laid in front of repair vehicles to keep them from sinking, and moving the tracked vehicles from one pole to the next often took hours. In many cases where the H-frame transmission structures had to be replaced it often took a full day.

Two weeks after the storm, the figures on the amount of material that SCE&G had used were available. This included:

Poles	5,435
Transformers	3,356
Wire	10,000,000 + feet
Crossarms	16,701
Insulators	43,506
Fuse Cutouts	117,637
Fuses	31,198

SCE&G's total loss was more than $1 billion, an amount almost equal to the market value of the company. Duke Power served three times the number of customers as SCE&G, and had twice the number of customers out of service.

―――――

Jennings Austin, the principal of Lincoln High School, had had no idea what he was getting into when he decided to stay at the school that day and help out with the evacuation. Shortly after noon he had casually strolled up and down the halls, checking to make sure everything was in order. He had already arranged for coffee and milk and sandwiches for more than a thousand people and had even added his own personal touch by getting packs of cards for the adults and board games for the kids. In addition, he had stocked up on plenty of candles and matches. Those, plus the auxiliary battery-operated lights near the ceiling, would be sufficient in case the power went out.

By four o'clock most of the crowd was in the cafeteria, more than six hundred people. About two hundred had gone to the gymnasium and the rest were in the home economics room, the band room, and a few classrooms. Before the night was over the total would be 1,145, ranging from infants to two-year-olds to the wheelchair-bound seventy-five-year-old Reverend Sheppard, pastor of the Baptist church. Jennings believed that the building was too strong to blow down and too well built for the roof to blow off, and he knew it was far enough back from the ocean. But even so, he still had a nagging feeling that something might slip up and go wrong.

At eleven o'clock, when the storm finally struck and the power went out, he had told his building superintendent to switch on the small emergency lights up in the corners of the cafeteria, in the gym, and out in the hallways. Things had gone smoothly, even in the darkness, even with everyone knowing that the storm was raging outside. No one had seemed worried. Small kids had still treated everything like a game and had been having more fun here than they would have had if they had been at home watching television.

The adults had been composed and almost nonchalant. Many had played cards and Monopoly by candlelight and flashlight, and the sense of calm had caught on everywhere. Only the tiny babies had made any outcry. Teenagers had their jam boxes going and many kids had literally danced their way through the first half of Hugo. Normally Jennings would have stopped them, but he had decided that if it would keep them entertained, he had no reason to do so unless it got out of hand. Everything had gone smoothly and the only precaution Jennings had even taken had been to go from room to room asking that everyone return to their families and stay with them until the storm was over. But now that little nagging feeling that had been bothering him earlier was coming back. Jennings had heard the wind whistling up under the roof and he could feel something in the air that he couldn't put his finger on.

It was right around one-thirty, right after the eye had just passed over, when the back side of Hugo hit them with all its fury and everything happened at once. The air-conditioning and heating units that lined the east wall blew in. Each one was three feet long

by two feet, and there were two in each one of the seven classrooms. Fourteen units all told.

Jennings was in the gymnasium when the water started coming
in. He had no idea where it was coming from; as far as he knew,
the building was watertight. For a moment, as he watched it rising
from the soles of his feet to the tops of his shoes, he just stood
there paralyzed with the possibilities and the dangers. He couldn't
move.

At first, some of the crowd and most of the small kids thought
the water spreading across the cafeteria floor was interesting, even
funny. Very few saw the danger. Soon it became a game, almost
like musical chairs, as they began sitting on the chairs and tables
and holding their feet up to keep them dry. But it was a game for
only a little while. In a few more minutes, the water was covering
the entire floor and it was still rising.

Jennings shook himself out of his trance and shouted for everyone to help get the small kids up on the stage at the end of the
room. As the adults and the teenagers carried the children across
the room, Jennings and three other men picked up Reverend Sheppard in his wheelchair and lifted him up with them. In the dim
glow from the tiny auxiliary lights, the Reverend and the kids on-
stage looked as if they were going to perform for the rest of the au-
dience, who were now climbing up on cafeteria tables.

Jennings, Deputy Charles DuTart, and his friend Edward Smith
had a quick conference. The water had risen above their knees and
was still rising. In almost no time it had risen more than two feet.
Sloshing to the end of the room and out of the hall, they went to
the main door to look outside. There was no power in McClellanville, but the lightning was flashing so fast that even the woods 300
yards away, across the parking lot, were lit up. As they stood there
peering through the narrow glass strip in the big door, a sudden
bolt of lightning made everything clear as day. And what Jennings
saw was almost too much to comprehend.

While the water inside the school was now between two and
three feet deep, outside it was over seven or eight—maybe even ten

feet. Pressing against the glass so he could see better, Jennings Austin saw something he would never have believed possible. Fish and shrimp were swimming around as if they were still in the ocean. As a matter of fact, they *were* still in the ocean, only now the ocean was a thousand yards inland from the shore. It was covering the parking lot and pushing against Lincoln High School and trying to get in. The only reason the water inside the school wasn't ten feet deep too was because the sturdy doors and windows were holding it back.

Elizabeth Brown, the school secretary, was with her daughter Sharon in the home economics room on the west side, the lee side of the building, with more than a hundred of the older people of McClellanville and most of the smaller children. Sharon was eight months pregnant, but for her and Elizabeth the storm didn't seem like much of a threat. Many of the adults had been in the room since that morning when the first warnings had come and they were still sitting around playing cards and Trivial Pursuit, oblivious to the flooding going on in the other rooms and in the cafeteria.

Quietly, and with no one seeing it at first, water began seeping in under the door. It began to spread but it was spreading so slowly that no one thought much about it. Finally Elizabeth, curious about where it was coming from, took a flashlight and went to the door that opened out onto the west side, the lee side of the building. The door had a six-inch-wide, three-foot-long glass pane running from the middle to the top. The lightning had stopped and it was pitch dark outside. Elizabeth put the flashlight up against the glass and pressed her face to it until she was used to the strange light. And then she saw it too.

At first she didn't believe it, either. It was like a dream, a nightmare. She was looking into water deeper than the door was tall and she was seeing exactly what Jennings had seen, fish and shrimp. Not wanting to panic the crowd, she whispered to Sharon to come over and take a look. Sharon gasped. Then they both realized that they were trapped.

But what could they do? Elizabeth remembered that there was a

way through a series of rooms and halls back to the cafeteria. But
she also remembered that the doors had been locked for security
reasons. Quickly she decided that if they were going to drown, they
were better off in the cafeteria with the rest of the people.

Elizabeth and Sharon led the group from one room to the next.
Each room was locked and they had to smash the glass with one of
the home economics class's irons and then reach in and open it.
After going through four or five classrooms, with the water getting
deeper and deeper, they finally came out at the cafeteria. But here
the surprise was almost as startling as seeing the fish and the
shrimp. The water was over four feet deep and every table and
chair in the room was floating! The crowd was packed together
up on the small stage at the end of the room. One of Elizabeth's
friends, Mary Wilson, was sitting on a big industrial-sized milk box
from the kitchen and using her hands like paddles, paddling herself
across the room and up to the stage.

Meanwhile, Jennings, Charles, and Edward had realized that with
the water rising so fast, the cafeteria and the whole school would
soon become a death trap. The water pressure would prevent anybody from getting out, and if they stayed inside they would certainly drown. By this time the water was four feet deep in the
cafeteria. Up on the low stage, which was only two feet above the
floor, the kids and the Reverend were perched on top of cafeteria
tables, looking out over the black water that was silently and relent-
lessly rising. Some of the adults had placed chairs on top of the tables. Only here was it dry, but even here, seven feet above the
floor, there was no safety. The small stage was getting smaller as it
got more and more crowded. To Jennings, nothing mattered now
but finding a way to get the crowd out of the cafeteria before it
flooded to the ceiling. He looked outside again, outside where the
fish were swimming and the waves were rising. In the flickering
green light he watched as car after car from the parking lot was
slammed against the building.

Jennings led the way as he, Charles, and Edward sloshed and
swam down the hall looking for a door they could open or a win-

dow they could break out. But every door they tried was backed up
with water and there was no budging them. Even with all three
pushing, there was no getting them open. They tried three windows, but the heavy safety plastic wouldn't crack either. Finally, in
a back classroom, Jennings remembered that a desk had been
shoved up under one of the big windows and that there was an
overhead projector near it. They swam into the room and, climbing
up on the desk, Edward, the biggest, began slamming the projector
against the top of the window. After five blows it finally gave way.

Jennings had played football in college and coached high school
ball, and he had stayed in good shape, so he was the first one out
of the top of the window. He levered himself up and onto the roof
and into the screaming wind and then helped the others up. The
plan was that once they were all up on the roof they would move
down toward the cafeteria. And here, forming a human chain, they
would smash in the top panels of the thirteen-foot windows and
start pulling the crowd out. It was the only solution—if there was
time.

The water was over five feet in the cafeteria now, and it was still
rising fast. If it reached seven feet, almost everyone, except the very
tallest who were standing on top of the tables, would be underwater. At ten and eleven feet, even the ones up on the stage, standing on chairs and on top of tables, would be underwater with
them. Jennings knew that unless they could break the cafeteria windows out and get the crowd out on the roof they would all drown.
But now there was another problem that they hadn't even considered. The wind was so strong that the men on the roof could barely
move. And every time they tried, it threatened to take them over
the side. Jennings grabbed a pipe as the wind sucked at him and
jerked him around violently. He was terrified and it was all he
could do just to hold on.

He saw now that there was no way in the world for him to get
down the roof to the cafeteria windows. And there was no way
back through the flooded hall. There was no way to do anything
but try and hold on. All he and Edward and Charles could do was

hang on and pray that a gust didn't tear their hands loose and fling them out into the dark water below. If the wind died down for a few minutes, maybe they could try the cafeteria plan, but for the moment all they could do was hold on.

The lightning kept flashing and they could see everything around them as if it were noon. A brick house a hundred yards from the school parking lot had been moved more than two hundred yards down the road. Live oaks and tall pines lay across one another and every one of the sixty-eight cars in the parking lot had been picked up and slammed against the school. Sixty- and seventy-foot-long mobile homes had been torn from their pads and were bobbing up and down in the surge like toy trains. A red pickup floated upside down, all four wheels spinning.

The green light stayed in the air and Jennings saw more than he wanted to see. He could actually measure the water as it rose up against the warehouse across the parking lot. He knew the warehouse was exactly twenty feet high and he could see that the water was over halfway up, over ten feet. It was not only rising, it was rising fast. It was useless, hopeless. He knew that in a few more minutes everyone in the school, almost the entire population of McClellanville, would drown.

And then he heard it. Under the wind, or off to one side of it, he heard the sound of screams. He listened close as he realized they were coming from the cafeteria. If they could scream they were alive. He held his breath and opened his mouth to hear better. But who could scream? Who was left? Maybe it was the ones on the stage on top of the chairs on top of the tables.

As Jennings Austin lay on the roof gripping the iron pipe and holding on for dear life, he prayed for the screaming to continue. But then the wind picked up and he lost it. Then it came back again, but this time it was fainter. It was thinning out and in his mind's eye he saw that only a few of the strong ones had survived. He could picture them trapped up at the ceiling and trying to breathe the last bit of the air. The others, the ones who hadn't already drowned, were holding on to anything that would float. For them, it was almost over. Soon they too would be pushed up against the ceiling where they would be trapped. And there they would be fighting one another for the space and the air or they would die from exhaustion and fear and simply give up and quietly sink.

The wind kept jerking Jennings around. Flying objects came skipping across the roof, hitting his head, his shoulders, his arms, and his legs. He tried to keep his face down and his eyes closed to protect them. As he lay there waiting for the wind to die down he was thinking about the people inside who couldn't swim. The ones who would panic and thrash out and try to cling to whoever was close. It was too horrible to even think about. As he lay there gripping the pipe, with his hands bleeding and his face raw and bruised from the beating he was taking from the shingles and branches and rocks, all he could do was silently pray.

It was almost two hours later before Hugo's winds began to slacken and finally pass over. Jennings, Charles, and Edward had clung to the same roof pipe, grimly listening for the screams that were no longer coming from the cafeteria. Jennings was sure that when they finally got back down inside, they were going to see a room filled with bodies. He had imagined that while a few might still be floating, most of them would have sunk to the floor. What could he do? What could he even begin to do? How could he even account for the fact that he was on the roof while his whole school drowned?

One hour before Jennings forced his way onto the roof, Captain Stan Salter had leaned over his wheel, trying not to collapse, and had drawn a long and profound sigh of relief. The eye of Hugo had finally come over. As he hung on the wheel, draped over it with exhaustion, he wondered how much longer he could keep it up. Salter, in his shrimp trawler, had climbed seventy-foot waves in the Atlantic that were so steep he thought he was going to tumble over backward. But they were nothing compared to what he had seen tonight. He'd never seen anything even close to it before, not even during his naval days in World War II, when he was in the invasion of the Philippines.

With the three big lights on the bow, he'd seen everything that had happened to the harbor, and it was a nightmare he would never get out of his mind. The initial blast of Hugo had taken the tin roofing from the fish houses, but the big damage was to the boats moored to the dock. The wind and roaring tide ripped some of them loose, tossing them around with so much force they looked like toy boats in a bathtub as they were sent tumbling and skidding up the river, over the banks, and out across the parking lot.

But now the eye was on them and Salter knew he could relax awhile. LeRoy served the stew cold to the crew, and Salter ate his standing at the wheel, watching and waiting for the back end of the storm. He'd watched Horace's and Joe's boats, tied down to the pier across from the *Mermaid,* make it through the front end of the storm. But now the back end, the killer end, was closing in and Salter knew a big tidal surge would come with it.

With his lights aimed far out into the bay, Salter didn't have long to wait. He heard it first, then he felt it. Then he saw it. Scraping his stew into the garbage, he dried his hands on his pants and grabbed the wheel. He knew this was it; he was just surprised it had come so fast. The wind picked up suddenly, as if it had been shoved, and in seconds it was back at full blast, with the waves slicing in, one on top of the other, and foam whipping off the whitecaps, spewing as high as he could see. Suddenly the full brunt hit and the tin roofs that had stayed in place during the front end were now being stripped and peeled away with a vengeance. And with the tin, everything else. First the tin, then the lathing, then the Sheetrock, and finally the two-by-four framing from the understructure of all the houses along the dock was ripped to splinters and shreds and sent sailing out over the village.

Salter was playing his three lights out over the harbor when he felt the boat shift. One of the bow lines had parted and the boat was coming around broadside to the storm. If it wasn't fixed in seconds, he and his crew were lost. It had to be replaced, but he knew it was going to take more than one or two men to go out in the incredible wind. He tied the wheel off, and with all three of his crew holding him, they inched out of the cabin and crossed the deck to get to the line. The spray was thick and filled with salt and sand and felt like tiny nails; the wind kept knocking all four of them around. They held on to each other tighter and shuffled forward inch by inch by inch. Finally they got to the bow and Salter changed the line; then they started the slow shuffle back to the cabin.

Salter was drenched and aching, and his hands were raw, when he got back in the cabin. He trained the lights out toward the ocean now, watching for the surge. At first he didn't know what he was looking for. And then he thought he saw something—a long, dark streak on the already dark water. His lights picked it up about a hundred yards out. It was a giant wave—the silent kind that came out of nowhere with no warning—the kind he'd heard about in the Indian Ocean; the wave that they called the tsunami. Hugo's tidal surge was just like that, silent, black, ominous.

Salter felt his skin crawl, and his chapped and burning hands turned white on the wheel. He knew the physics of the tidal surge; that for every foot of water there were two hundred square miles of water behind it, pushing it forward. And for a twenty-foot wave— the mathematics of energy for *that* equation was a hundred times stronger than all the atomic bombs that had ever been exploded. He watched it, fascinated by it, and recalled a line that Rocky Graziano delivered after he was knocked out by Sugar Ray Robinson. He'd said, "I saw it coming, but since I had no way of getting out of the way, I just watched it with a deep and profound admiration."

It hit and Stan Salter and his crew were thrown across the cabin. Each grabbed a rope as the boat rose up in the air, five feet, ten feet, fifteen feet. The *Mermaid* was making a deep, tearing, groaning noise but the lines held and the big barge's weight kept it still. Salter recovered, and checking to make sure the engine was still running in full reverse and none of the lines had fouled the prop, he

swung his lights out over the fish house, the pier, and the shrimp
boats that were tied up along the dock.

And then he saw something he couldn't believe: the end of the
dock had come loose from its pilings and was beginning to rise into
the air. Then it was the whole dock. It kept rising until it was standing almost straight up, all fifty or sixty feet of it, and it stood there
trembling, balanced between some lunatic forces that Salter found
incomprehensible. And as it stood there, the six boats tied to it, one
by one, simply dropped off. One was Horace's, one was Joe's. Salter
knew how hard they had worked to buy their boats and he hated
what he was seeing. The boats dropped off and hit the water,
bounced once, and were picked up by the surge and tossed like
Frisbees up the creek and out into the woods. Stan followed the
boats with his lights and saw Horace's, the *Olly May,* come to rest
on top of the Jenkinses' house. The bottom was stove in, the outriggers snapped, and the propeller was sticking straight up in the air.
The Jenkinses' roof collapsed under it.

The surge picked Joe's boat straight up and sent it sailing across
the parking lot and up the road until it vanished in the thick trees
and kudzu vine, three hundred yards from the dock. And then another boat that seemed to come out of nowhere rammed into the
Olly May, completely destroying the boat and the house.

Salter slowly realized that what he was seeing was something absolutely terrible. He was watching the utter and the complete destruction of his village of McClellanville.

PART THREE

Friday Morning

12 ⟿

Behind the Dunes

Many scientists will argue that hurricanes are the actual creators of life as we know it, and they make a good case for it. Their reasoning runs that in the beginning, some four billion years ago, the atmosphere was one raging, boiling storm that thundered and circled over the earth's surface in much the same manner that the winds, we are now told, circle Mars. In some unknown manner, the storm's endless bolts of lightning gradually worked a change on the few basic elements in the atmosphere, causing them to be energized into complex organic compounds that drifted down onto the planet's warm waters. It was here in this nutrient broth that the compounds developed in complexity and, after linking with other compounds, eventually gave rise to protoplasms capable of reproducing and developing into still more complex forms of life. It was out of this that life, from the lowest algae and tadpole to the largest dinosaur and, ultimately, man, evolved.

Today we view the hurricane as a source of destruction and destruction only. This, however, is only from our perspective. While the storm certainly destroys, it can at the same time actually rebuild—replacing and restoring the land that has been paved over and "developed" along rivers and beachfronts. And, probably more importantly, it can force us to examine more closely the damage that we have brought upon ourselves long before the storms.

Beach developers, much like AK-47 owners, are notorious when it comes to preaching the gospel that America is still a free country and using that gospel to justify selfish agendas:

a person should have the right to build a house, a condo, a golf course, or a seawall, wherever he chooses—on the beach, on the wetlands, anywhere—as long as he pays for it. What they are saying, in effect, is that erosion and damage to the eco-system are private problems, ones that can be solved and paid for by the beachfront owners. Environmentalists take a longer view, looking at more than the immediate acreage and a twenty-year mortgage. They maintain that the developers are taking advantage of weak laws and weaker enforcement by building seawalls, or as they call them, "sea armor," and are building too close to the water—in many cases right on the dunes. In the process, they have created a long-range erosion problem that will last for generations. Most geologists and coastal scientists now hold that one of the greatest causes of beach erosion is that seawalls don't allow the sand to shift and restore itself.

Fortunately, the law, like the coastline, is changing. With the encouragement of environmentalists and the cooperation between the tourist industry and state government, we are actually in the process of changing the rules to accommodate the new way we are viewing beach development, the wetlands, and seawalls.

South Carolina's tourism industry has realized that the fu-ture of tourism in the state lies in taking a firm stand against old laws that allowed developers much too much latitude in building on the beachfront. One critic of beach overdevelop-ment, State Sen. James Waddell of the Coastal Council, the governing body that oversees the coast and the wetlands in the state, said, "the state has given few accommodations to the tourist industry. Tourism is the number two industry in the state, and frankly, I think it will be number one in a couple of years." He went on to say that the state has for too many years allowed developers to do pretty much what they pleased. But all this has now changed. The new laws move away from the old concept, which held that property rights were above everything, to a stronger ecological view that the public beaches must be preserved.

Orrin Pilkey, a controversial coastal geologist from Duke University who has attacked development policies all up and down the Atlantic Coast, praised a recent ruling by the South Carolina Supreme Court in support of the new laws. "South Carolina can take pride in taking firmer steps than almost any other state in the nation to protect its coast," Pilkey said.

Many opinion-makers seem to share such attitudes. Here, under the headline "Big Win for Taxpayers and the Environment," is the editorial that appeared on February 14, 1991, in *The State*:

> Three years ago with the passage of the landmark Beach-front Management Act, the General Assembly took a giant step towards protecting one of South Carolina's most precious natural resources. With its historic ruling Monday, the S.C. Supreme Court validated the prudence and prescience of that legislative action.
>
> . . . In passing the law three years ago [the year before Hugo hit], the General Assembly properly determined that extraordinary steps were needed to protect the state's 180-mile coastline, an area rich in plant and wildlife and a center of tourism, from critical erosion, a natural process exacerbated by construction of buildings close to the beaches and sand dunes.
>
> The seriousness of the problem was made alarmingly apparent when Hurricane Hugo barged ashore with monster winds in September of '89. More than anything, the storm alerted all to the vulnerability of the state's delicate ecosystem.
>
> Property owners' suits notwithstanding, the 1988 Beach-front Management Act—and amendments to it passed last year—is reasonable and well within the legitimate police power of the state. It allows limited construction in an area

20 feet landward of the dune line—the so-called dead zone—
but bans the construction of new seawalls and strictly regu-
lates the reconstruction of existing seawalls in the event of
damage.

Additionally, it gives the Coastal Council regulatory au-
thority to protect other environmentally sensitive areas, such
as the tidal flats and other wetlands. The Supreme Court's
endorsement of the act is a victory for the state's taxpayers.
More significantly, it is a triumph for the environment over
indiscriminate development.

Hugo wasn't entirely responsible for this court decision, but
there is little doubt that the terrible damage to the Isle of
Palms, Sullivan's Island, and Pawley's Island, and the virtual
wiping out of the beachfronts at Garden City, Surfside Beach,
Murrell's Inlet, and South Myrtle Beach, probably fueled the
fire that was already there. Certainly the developers can't be
held responsible for this disaster, but over the years their actions seem to have done much to exacerbate it. By cutting
through and leveling the old dunes, by destroying the ground
cover, by building seawalls that worsen erosion, and by paving
every possible square yard for more construction, more golf
courses, and more parking, they certainly did very little to
discourage the destructive power of 150-mph winds.

A 150-mph wind roaring across a developed area that has
been stripped of dunes and ground cover is so strong that it's
almost impossible to imagine. A medium-sized person standing up will be picked up and flung into the air like so much
cardboard. A person lying down facing the wind will start
moving along the ground faster and faster until he or she is
tumbling over and over and bouncing along completely out of
control. Even solid concrete, when hit with this much water-
laden wind, will begin dissolving and crumbling in much the
same manner a sugar cube will when sprayed. Nothing is sa-
cred, nothing is safe. With this in mind, it is hard to imagine

how terrible the winds must have been between midnight and three in the morning out on the Isle of Palms and Sullivan's Island.

Roscoe and Mike sat on the porch steps, looking out on the great calm that had descended around them. The waves had stopped, the ocean had smoothed out and the water, which had been eight to ten feet deep under the house, had receded and dropped to less than a foot. Above them the clouds parted, and a moment later there was a sky so clear, so calm, and so peaceful they could see the moon and the brilliant wash of the Milky Way. They didn't have any idea they were sitting in the middle of the hurricane's eye.

Mike said, "Man, oh, man, am I glad that son of a bitch is over. Was that the hurricane or what?"

Roscoe lay back on the porch looking straight up at the beautiful sky above. "I tell you one damn thing. I'm glad that sucker's over, too."

Roscoe had his hands behind his head and the heel of his right foot balanced on the toe of his left. The air was calm and balmy, and the temperature was rising so fast he took off his shirt. "Man, this is the life."

The only thing wrong was that Buckles wouldn't shut up. He was scratching the floor, as if there were something underneath, and whining. Roscoe had already given him all the bacon. "What do you want, boy? Come here." He patted his leg and whistled, but Buckles wasn't coming.

Roscoe stretched and yawned. "We've got to put that beer back or we're going to be in deep shit."

Mike agreed. "But look at it this way, at least we saved their dog. Come here, boy," he said, patting the step for the dog to come, but he still wouldn't budge. "Hey, Buckles," he raised his voice. "Make like that dog in that commercial and bring me and Roscoe another beer."

A breeze drifted over them and Roscoe raised his arms to cool his armpits. "Hey, now that feels good. You want to do something cool? Let's drag a couple mattresses out here and catch some sleep."

"I don't know, man. Look at those clouds."

Low clouds were drifting in and hiding the houses down the beach. Up the beach and out across the island it was still clear.

"Man, let's at least try it," Roscoe said. "We'll have a couple beers and just kick back."

They got up and went to pull the two big foam mattresses out of the guest bedroom. When they returned, Mike said, "Damn, look at those clouds. You can't even see the moon now."

"Mike," Roscoe said, "you worry too much. See that sliver? Look, you see it? Watch, it'll come back. Hell, give it a minute."

They lay back on the mattresses with their beers, watching the moon sliding in and out of the low clouds. Suddenly it felt colder. Then, just as suddenly, the clouds came together and the moon was gone. The slot of sky above them had closed and what looked and felt like a rainstorm was on them.

Mike laughed. "Worry, my ass. We're going to drown out here."

Roscoe was on his feet. "Let's get this crap inside." As they were shoving the mattresses through the sliding door, a powerful gust wrenched them out of their hands so fast they couldn't hold on. Then, just as fast, both mattresses were flipped over and blown over the sides of the deck and went sailing off into the dark, down the beach. "Damn!" Roscoe yelled.

They scrambled inside. The wind was blowing so hard it took both of them to close the door. Buckles was jumping around them, glad they were inside but still whining and making little yipping noises. It wasn't until they were inside that they looked back out at the ocean. What they saw froze them. The water was coming at them again but this time it was higher, much higher. It was more than five feet, more than ten—there was no telling how high it was. They rushed back to their posts at the window, pressing against it, knowing that if it went, they'd probably go with it.

With the flashlight lying on the floor trained on the tidal surge
rushing toward them, they pushed on the straining window. Mike
turned and looked over his shoulder. "Oh God! Not again."

Roscoe glanced back and saw the linoleum ballooning up again.
"Sheeeeit."

He spun back around to see the surf. The water was black as ink
and coming at them like a moving cliff. He'd never seen anything
like it; not even in the movies, not even in the surfing magazines.
There was nothing to do but hold on and hold on. And then he saw
another wave behind the first one. It kept rising and kept getting
taller and bigger and stronger as it crossed the dunes and he realized, as it reared up and rolled over them, that the little stilted
house didn't have a chance.

Roscoe had just enough time to hook the flashlight onto his belt
and grab Buckles's collar when the full force of the wave slammed
into the house with an impact that rocked it back on its sixteen-
foot stilts. The house stayed in that position as the roof peeled back
like the lid of a sardine can, and water, sand, seaweed, and fish
poured in through the enormous opening. The left side of the house
seemed to just fall off. Only the front was standing, completely un-
supported. Then the window shattered and collapsed, and the floor
beneath them gave way like a trap door.

For a split second the boys seemed to hang in the air. Then they
dropped straight down. Straight down into the black water, where
they were picked up and slammed around by a hydraulic force so
strong they couldn't even breathe. Their arms and legs were flailing
as they were smashed into the ground, then snatched up, hurled
out, and smashed down again. Roscoe tried to hold onto Buckles,
but the surge was too strong. He broke away. It was like surfing in
whitewater rapids. They lost all control. One second they were upside down, the next backwards, the next on top of one another and
rolling along with a Hurby Kurby garbage container, a screen door,
and what looked like a plastic chaise longue. All that mattered was
breathing and protecting their eyes. They held their hands in front

of their faces as the ocean swept them back across the island. They had no idea if they were heading toward high ground or being taken out to sea.

The water seemed freezing cold, but they were too scared and too busy to notice. They skidded and tumbled and rode the salty water for one hundred yards, two hundred yards. At one point Roscoe felt the ground, but there was no way to stop and nowhere to stand. Again, they bumped into each other, but again, the current was too strong and moving too fast. Buckles kept banging into them, too, but he was too slick and they couldn't get a grip on him either.

They were sucked under again for what seemed like a full minute. They surfaced and rose up, gasping, only to be sucked back down again. It was like being caught in a raging surf, but it was fifty times stronger, and it was pitch dark and terrifying. They were still rolling and tumbling and had no idea how far they were traveling.

Roscoe knew that the big danger was something hitting them. But his hands were free to protect his head and he kept them there, and he kept getting ready to tuck his knees up tight and roll, as he'd learned from the surfing magazines. A big ceiling beam struck them both at once, but it was traveling in the same direction and didn't hurt. If it had come from the other direction, it would have killed them. A white Volkswagen came tumbling by, end over end, and for a split second Roscoe thought of climbing in. But then he knew it would be impossible to open the door. Something hit him hard in the middle of his back and drove him down. He held onto it so it wouldn't hit him again. It was the Century 21 real estate sign.

Then, miraculously, they were washed up on the floating roof of a house and Buckles was with them. He couldn't stand on the pitched roof, with the water rocking it, and Mike pushed him onto his stomach with his front paws over one side and his back over the other. He settled down while Roscoe and Mike pulled seaweed and long strands of kelp from their hair and unwound it from their necks and arms. Mike petted him and kept shouting, "That a boy! Good boy! Good boy!"

The pitch dark suddenly turned light. It was that same eerie phosphorescent green again. Sides of houses, roofs of houses, and whole houses slid by in the weird and pulsing light that was now backlit by the blinding flashes of lightning. What looked like an entire white picket fence with the swinging gate intact came sailing by at a wicked angle and wrapped around a big floating tree. It was like a nightmare. A backlit, lightning-strobed nightmare that would only end when everything standing was destroyed. Window screens were everywhere, along with refrigerators, television sets, electric lines, tables, lamps, phones, shower curtains. All around them, whole houses had fallen completely apart and everything from dishes and magazines to shirts and shoes and the morning paper came swirling by as the boiling surge made its trip across the narrow island.

They clung to the roof for less than two minutes before another wave sank it. Then they were back out in the water. They traveled another twenty to thirty yards and stopped, draped over a big limb in a tree that had fallen. But this time Buckles was lost. Another tree floated by with a screeching cat high in its branches, and Roscoe knew he would never forget the sound. He was frantically looking around for Buckles.

The wind kept changing keys, as shrill as a single piccolo one second, as deep as a hundred bassoons the next. The sounds ran together as the careening wind moved through a spectrum of speeds that no one could measure. And there were other sounds even more frightening. The worst was the deadly buzzing, whirring sounds of the tin roofs and the electric lines cutting through the air. Roscoe and Mike clung to the branch, praying it would hold. But soon it gave a violent shudder, shook again, and they were plunged back into the rushing water. Once again they were tumbling to the bottom one minute, skimming along the top the next. Once again they were rolling and somersaulting along, completely out of control.

Finally they landed on another roof. They were trying to straddle the peak when Buckles banged into them. He was whimpering and shaking, but he was wagging his tail. They both held on to the chimney and they both held onto the dog. Roscoe unhooked the flashlight and played the beam out over the black water, looking for the cat that had gone howling by. But now he couldn't find the tree. The house was making a terrible groaning noise as if it were being twisted from underneath. He began counting the cars that went by. It was three, then he added the Volkswagen and made it four.

The sights around them were unbelievable. Trees kept sliding by with their branches filled with clothes and window screens, rugs and picket fences. Roscoe kept sweeping the light over everything, looking for people, but there was no sign of anyone. It was as if they were at the edge of the world, or the end of it, or on another planet. He'd never been so scared in his entire life. "You okay?" he yelled to Mike.

Mike yelled back. "Scared!"

They crouched on the roof, trying to get as low as they could to keep out of the way of flying objects. But there was no escape, and shingles and clamshells and every conceivable small object, from rocks and shoes to bottlecaps and beer cans, were pounding on their heads and hands and shoulders. Buckles, spread-eagled over the peak of the roof, couldn't get any leverage to do anything but whine and make his pathetic little yipping sound.

The clouds that came in from the ocean were racing at them at ground level, and the sky kept changing from gray to black, from black to green. Every few minutes it would light up with a white light that looked like ten thousand flashbulbs. Roscoe, still playing his flashlight beam over everything that passed, yelled, "Look at that!" About thirty feet away two terrorized cats and three chickens floated by in a tree. Then he saw the snakes. It looked like four or five dozen. They were on the low limbs; he'd seen their red eyes first, and then their long black and yellow bodies. They were moccasins, cottonmouth water moccasins. He kept the beam on them as if it would keep them away. Then the tree slowly began rolling over, taking with it the cats, the chickens, and the snakes.

A coil of rope came by and Roscoe shuddered, thinking it was another snake. Then he reached out and grabbed it, almost losing Buckles. He tied a slipknot and looped it around the dog, then he wrapped it around and around the steel chimney.

Then, cupping his hand to Mike's ear, he yelled, "I think Don's going to forget that beer!" He didn't feel like joking, but he was so scared he had to say something.

Mike nodded. Then he said, "I'm scared, Roscoe."

"Yeah, same here." He forced a grin. "Some tide, hey?"

But Mike didn't even hear him.

All around them the debris, which seemed to be coming from every direction, was piling up on the roof. Just below there were deck chairs, a picnic table, a Raggedy Ann doll, and a stop sign. A line of Gamecock plastic cups came by as if they were tied together on a string, followed by a bookcase filled with books and records and a mailbox with a robin painted on the side. Whole sections of roofs and window casements were piling up, and three white ducks that had drowned came by one after the other in a single file as if they were still following one another.

The wind kept screaming and the waves kept pounding. The rumble and the groaning of the house beneath them sounded almost human. Despite the stupefying force of the wind and the bombardment of shingles, oyster shells, fish, screens, and kitchenware, they clung to the chimney like animals, with every ounce of energy they had.

At one point they felt the wind drop for a few seconds and the sound die down. It was as if the eye were coming over again. But it wasn't the eye; it was something else. Something more frightening. A vacuum pocket had formed over them. The lull grew calmer. The wet hair on Buckles's back was straight up and he kept yipping. Roscoe was shaking so hard he could hear his teeth chattering.

And then the pocket passed and the winds struck again, even

stronger. They grabbed each other's arms and held onto the chimney as they were lifted up and stretched out like washing on a clothesline and whipped from side to side. A clap of thunder boomed and a giant mound of water, like a gigantic pyramid, rose up and pounded them down so hard and so flat that the sandpaper texture of the shingles was stamped on their faces. Roscoe thought his ribs were broken. Just as quickly as it had appeared, the wave vanished. Roscoe looked over at Mike to say something, but Mike was pointing and screaming, "My God!"

It was a tornado, coming right at them. Roscoe saw it, then he heard it, then he saw it again. Then he saw it too clearly as the lightning flashed and lit up the whole eastern sky, backlighting it as it came angling in across the water toward them. Roscoe knew it was all over and, wrapping one arm around Mike and the other around the chimney and pushing as hard as he could against Buckles, he closed his eyes and kept saying, "Oh Jesus. Oh Jesus. Oh Jesus."

Something metallic screamed out of the air, something Roscoe couldn't make out, but it tipped his ear as it flew right past his face. Suddenly the tornado was gone and Mike was screaming, "Did you see that thing? Did you see it?"

Roscoe was numb with fright. The tornado had come out of nowhere, no warning, nothing. All he could do was shake his head and say, "Damn. Damn." His teeth were chattering and there was nothing he could do to make them stop. His muscles were aching from holding on so hard. Then he saw what had happened. "Oh my God! Buckles! He's gone. Jesus!"

The rope was still wrapped around the chimney, only now the other end was frayed, just hanging there. Roscoe held onto the steel pipe. "Oh Jesus, he's gone. That poor bastard's out there, drowned." And for the first time that night, he and Mike cried.

Then, almost as quickly as the tornado had appeared, the wind slackened and almost stopped. They were able to talk without having to shout. Roscoe was drying his eyes. "I think it's over. I swear to God, I really think it's over."

Mike nodded his head up and down. "Boy, I hope so." He was still crying about Buckles. "Boy, I really hope so."

Roscoe tried to grin. "Well, it's exactly like I said. You take a high tide and then a storm and anything can happen."

Mike pretended he was going to hit him but he was too weak to even raise his arm.

Roscoe wiped his eyes with the back of his arm. "Oh, man. I hate it. That dog going like that."

Finally the wind stopped and for a few minutes it was as if there had never been a storm at all. Roscoe stood up and after he stretched, he balanced on the point of the roof and unzipped his jeans.

"This is the first leak I've taken since that damn thing started."

Mike joined him, laughing. "Same here. Damn, am I glad it's over. You know who's really going to be mad? Jay and Billy. Wait until we tell them what happened out here. Hey, you know your ear is bleeding?"

Roscoe felt it and shrugged. "It's only a scratch."

They were quiet again and then Roscoe said, "Damn. I feel bad. That was a really great dog."

The fair weather didn't last. The wind picked up, the temperature dropped, and the rain started again. Roscoe and Mike wrapped their arms around their legs and, with their chins on their knees, they faced east and began the long wait until daylight.

13 ⇒

Picking Up the Pieces

While only the fringe of Hugo hit Columbia, the damage was considerable. "The Bubble," the indoor athletic field at the University of South Carolina, was flattened, power was out in half the city for a week, and more than two hundred cars were damaged by falling trees. Camden, 30 miles east, reported winds of 110 mph and the beautiful Robert Mills Courthouse, the centerpiece for Camden, was badly damaged. But the worst disaster would be to the mobile home owners; here the figures were staggering. Of the three thousand units in the Camden area, almost 90 percent were completely destroyed. Florence, 70 miles east of Columbia (and where hundreds of people from the coast had fled for safety), was hit with almost the full force of the storm, as was Charlotte, more than 220 miles from Hugo's landfall in Charleston.

The governor committed the National Guard early to the tasks of maintaining law and order before and after the storm and assisting with the massive cleanup. Maj. Gen. T. Eston Marchant, the state's adjutant general, said that more than 7,000 guardsmen were committed—nearly half of the state's combined force. "Even with all the warning and the full anticipation that Hugo would strike South Carolina," Marchant said, "you couldn't possibly realize the devastation until looking at the aftermath."

Thousands of guardsmen were in their home armories when the storm struck. When morning came it was their job to get to the towns that needed them most. "We literally cut our way into the Charleston area," said Lt. Col. Frank Chapman, who commanded one Guard unit. "We cleared the roads as we went. It took four or five hours to cover a ten- or twenty-mile stretch of road at times."

Out on the Isle of Palms the Guard had the terrible task of telling irate residents that they could not go back out to their homes until the island was made secure. The dangers of gas explosions caused by butane and propane tanks ripping loose was too great, and the Guard had to stop them at the Ben Sawyer Bridge.

While there were problems with crowds out on the Isle of Palms and Sullivan's Island, Charleston had it worse. Staff Sgt. Bill Petty stood duty and fought back tears as 3,000 people pushed and shoved and even slugged it out to buy fifty-pound bags of ice for six dollars. "People were begging for the ice," he said. On one particular day, people lined up at 6 A.M. to buy the ice; by 2 P.M., the ice was gone and 500 people remained.

Staff Sgt. James Sugart of Lockhart had the disconcerting job of pulling night patrol in the streets of Charleston, where total darkness dominated the city for many nights. "It's scary out there. You don't know what to expect. There are no lights. You don't see anything."

The main fear was looting, and the Guard stationed personnel at every corner with fixed bayonets and live ammunition. Reuben Greenberg, the chief of police of Charleston, had already issued the order that his men were to "beat the hell out of looters instead of arresting them, because there's no more room in the jails."

Brig. Gen. Frank Jones, who commanded the Guard's task force in Charleston, was confident that looting was held to an absolute minimum by the Guard's presence. "I feel confident the show of force we've had, in conjunction with civilian law enforcement personnel, has been helpful in deterring looting," he said.

In any event, the looting was minimal in Charleston. On up

the beach, at Surfside Beach and Garden City, northeast of Charleston along the coast, the residents weren't quite so lucky. Here the guardsmen were busy keeping the roads clear and delivering generators and food. A few looters with four-wheel-drive equipment came down along the shore from Myrtle Beach and plundered oceanfront homes, taking television sets, stereos, and anything that they could carry. Fortunately, this stopped soon when the Guard found out about it.

In the days and weeks following the storm, the National Guard was widely praised for maintaining law and order, clearing roads, delivering and operating generators, delivering supplies, flying damage assessment missions, rebuilding causeways, providing heavy equipment, and establishing communication lines. In the Virgin Islands, seven Air National Guardsmen from the 240th Combat Communication Squadron provided the vital first communication link between the ravaged islands and U.S. government officials on the mainland.

Up in Camden, where the Guard stayed for over two weeks, the Camden School of Hair Design, to show its appreciation, spent a couple of hours one weekend night at the Camden Armory, giving the guardsmen haircuts. And one resident out on Folly Beach made sure people knew his feelings. On the plywood that boarded up the windows to the beachfront house were the words, "Thank you, Jesus. Also Thanks N' Guards."

Back in Columbia, by eleven o'clock, the winds were rising. The electricity had gone out and everyone had gone from sitting comfortably in front of J.C.'s thirty-six-inch Sony to huddling around Roscoe's little portable, which would only get CBS. Everyone, including Olly May, was drinking by now but everyone was stone sober. Dan Rather's reports kept coming in every thirty minutes, and other than that it was "The Andy Griffith Show." In the meantime, Max was on the phone with a friend in Atlanta who was telling him what CNN was reporting. Max, in turn, had relayed the news to the room. "Jesus Christ! Can you believe this? The Ben Sawyer Bridge is spinning around and going down!"

Olly May asked, "What bridge is that?"

"The one to Sullivan's Island," Tracy said, as she reached over to pat Elise's leg. She knew she was frantic about Roscoe.

"God!" Max covered the speaker. "Okay, y'all, the bridge has just broken off. It's in the water and no one can get off that stupid place."

Elise shivered and gripped her fingers together. Tracy tried to hug her but she pulled away. Tracy said, "They'll be fine, hon. That house is solid as a rock."

Don wasn't paying attention to anything but Dan Rather, who had come back on for a minute, but the picture was shrinking and was now down to the size of a cigarette pack. Don said, "The batteries are going. Elise, y'all got any more?"

She shook her head and wiped her eyes. "No, I'm afraid not."

Max had hung up from his call to Atlanta and was pulling one of J.C.'s raincoats out of the hall closet. "I'll pull the car up. Maybe we can hear the radio."

Tracy frowned. "Max, don't you dare go out there. You'll get hit by something."

In his best John Wayne delivery, Max said, "Honey, old Duke don't mind a few things falling. Hell, you should have seen what we were up against out in old El Paso."

Outside, the first thing Max did was give his car a quick inspection. There wasn't a scratch on the car or a drop of water on the custom red leather interior. He drove it slowly over the lawn and the ivy up as close to the window as he could get. Then he tuned his radio to 560 AM, where Andy Thomas came blaring out through his quadrophonic speakers. He pushed the button for the right window, opening it halfway. Then after he draped J.C.'s coat over the part of the seat that would get wet, he hightailed it back into the house. As he closed the door a horrendous crash shook the whole house.

Tracy came running into the hall, with everyone following.

"What was that?"

"It must've been a tree," Max said.

Don, who was standing at the window, just stood there. Then he turned to Max with his shoulders slumped and his palms up. "Sorry, old man."

Tracy wailed. "Oh, my God! Max! Your beautiful car! It's flat!"

Max shrunk from the window and shook his head. "And I just finished paying for it." He tried to smile. "But listen to that radio." And then, in a thin, shaky voice, with absolutely no conviction, "You know something? You just can't beat quality."

While they were all standing at the window looking at the car and listening to Andy Thomas on Max's radio, another noise shook the house. It was from the back. The magnolia tree had fallen on the porch and one big branch had crashed through the hall and into the kitchen. The wind was howling through the roof and after it had blown out every candle in the house it proceeded to rip and shred every piece of paper on the table and counter tops and every poster off the walls.

A few hours later, with dawn in the sky and the storm past, Elise and Tracy, seeing that the Askins across the street still had power, went out to ask if they would run their lawnmower extension cord over as far as it would go. In the middle of the street Elise and Tracy made the connection to a long utility cord they'd found in J.C.'s garage, then they dragged the heavy orange line into the house and plugged it into the television set.

It was getting brighter outside and the news helicopters were already flying over Charleston and Mt. Pleasant. They kept showing footage of the Ben Sawyer Bridge, with one end sticking straight up in the air, and of boats from the Charleston Marina that had washed over four hundred yards from their moorings, and had come to rest in the middle of Lockwood Avenue. The helicopter cameras were also showing the big section of tin roof that had peeled back from City Hall. There was no news of McClellanville, and none of Sullivan's Island.

Don, Tracy, Olly May, and Elise stayed glued to the television set, hoping, and at the same time not hoping, for some shots of the beachfront of Sullivan's Island or news from McClellanville. Finally the cameras zoomed in on the Isle of Palms, only a few miles north of Sullivan's. Tracy gasped. "Jesus! Look!"

It looked as if the entire development had been destroyed. Roofs and sides of houses, whole boats and pieces of furniture were stacked up twenty and thirty feet, and when the camera panned down one stretch of beach, every house on the front line was gone. Whole houses were washed out onto the Wild Dunes Links Course, along with sailboats and motorboats. The front of a long, white screen porch, complete with a door, had wrapped itself around a telephone pole and was moving up and down with the tide. On the golf course it looked as if every tree had fallen. The seventeenth and eighteenth holes, two of the most famous and most photographed holes in the country, had been completely washed away. The rest of the course was under six feet of saltwater.

The helicopter and the camera turned away from Wild Dunes and started down the beach toward Sullivan's Island, about four miles south. Elise could hardly stand it. She was holding her breath, praying as fast as she could that Don and Tracy's house would be intact and the boys would be there on the sun deck waving up at the camera.

Tracy was so nervous she couldn't stop pointing and couldn't stop talking. She sounded like she was giving a guided tour. "There's the Maynards' place. It looks okay. But where's the Palmers'? They should be next door. Oh Jesus! Oh Jesus, it's gone. And the Peterses' and the Boyds'. Oh my God, they're all gone. They're all gone." She was sitting on the couch, bouncing up and down and waving her hands. "Look! Look, two, three, four houses in a row that haven't even been touched. Lord, none of this makes any sense."

The beachfront was like a battlefield that had been ripped apart by heavy artillery fire. Three or four houses in a row were missing, then two or three in a row would be standing. Others were still there but looked as if they had exploded or simply collapsed in on themselves. The only pattern was that there was no pattern. Elise got up and stood behind the couch; she was having trouble breathing. At any moment she expected to see two unidentified bodies lying facedown in the sand and she knew they would be Roscoe and Mike. Olly May was pacing back and forth.

Tracy kept trying to make it make sense as the camera eye slid inexorably down the beach, getting closer and closer to their place. Their pink house would be unmistakable. Either it would be there, or it wouldn't. Then she saw what she thought was a pattern; all of the houses that were built on cement pads were gone; the only ones standing were the ones that were built on pilings. She whispered this to Don: their house might be okay. He nodded, but he wasn't listening; he was too intent, watching the screen.

Tracy gripped his hand as the helicopter came down the beach. "I can't stand this!" He grabbed her arm and whispered fast, "Just calm down. It's going to be okay."

She pressed close. "You promise and guarantee?"

Don said, "Yes, I promise."

"Well, say it, say it right. And don't forget Buckles."

Don nodded, still watching the screen. "I promise and guarantee that our house will not be touched by Hugo. As a matter of fact, I don't think it's going to even scratch it. And old Buckles is going to be fine too."

Tracy squirmed and twisted her hands. "Oh God, it's getting so close. There's the Pooles' place and it hasn't even been touched. Maybe we're okay."

Don nodded slowly, "Of course we are. We're up sixteen damn feet."

But the next three houses were completely gone and the fourth had skidded back almost a hundred yards out across the road. The fifth was coming up on the edge of the picture, then the sixth, and beyond that was the seventh, which was theirs.

Tracy blurted out, "We're next! Oh my God, we're next."

Everyone leaned forward as the camera moved slowly down the next one hundred feet. Then everyone gasped.

There was no pink house, just an empty lot with black pilings pointing backward toward the bay at a thirty-degree angle. Wedged up against the pilings was the white leather couch Tracy had bought in Atlanta, and wrapped around one of the arms, its tail blowing in the wind, was the fishnet she'd decorated with shells and seaweed, that had hung from the ceiling.

Elise was crying and shaking her head from side to side. "The kids. No, it can't be. . . ." She couldn't go on.

At first light, around seven, Roscoe and Mike slid down from the roof and started wading through the water for the nearest house. They wanted to find a phone and they were hungry. They were also cold and wet; all night they'd been freezing in their blue jeans and T-shirts, huddled against the wind. As they sloshed through the knee-high water and the mud, they kept looking around, hoping to see Buckles perched on some rooftop waiting for them. But it looked like the whole island had been ruined. What lay around them looked like a giant landfill, with everything piled in on top of everything else. A few houses were still standing, but most of them had been ripped apart and carried to the far side of the island, where they lay stacked up along with the cars, small boats, furniture, mattresses, and even shower curtains.

A hundred yards or so up the beach they saw a house high up on pilings, with the back blown out, and they headed for it. Up close it looked like a dollhouse, the kind with one side open so you could reach in and move the furniture around, or set a table, or make a bed. Other than the back being ripped off, the house looked as if it had escaped the storm. They rushed to it, shimmied up what was left of the stair rails, and went inside.

Miraculously, everything in the house was dry. Standing in the kitchen, they looked out the back at the devastated houses, the broken and fallen trees, and the endless piles of refrigerators, washing machines, and television sets that seemed to go on forever. Roscoe said, "Man, you realize we lived through that?"

Mike nodded. "I can't believe any of this. I swear I can't."

The first thing they did was check the phone. It was dead. In the bathroom they found a stack of thick beach towels and, after stripping off their clothes, they rubbed themselves down, shivering. Then, wrapping the towels around their waists and shoulders, they went into the bedroom and started going through the closets.

In a few minutes they found two Day-Glo–orange sweatsuits. Roscoe held his out, examining the white paws that covered the shirt and the pants. "Clemson! Man, I can't wear this." But he slipped the shirt over his head, and after pulling on the pants he opened the refrigerator. "Damn, no beer. I was all set for a nice cold one."

Mike grimaced. "Oh, come off it. If they had it you wouldn't touch it, and you know it." He looked in over Roscoe's shoulder. "Hey! They've got peanut butter, and there's chicken. Man, they got chocolate milk here. I wish we could heat it up."

Later, as they were eating out on the sun deck, a helicopter flew over and dipped down to take a long look at them. They thought maybe it had a television camera on it, so they waved and did a little disco dance. They even bowed.

"Maybe Cindy will be watching when this comes on," Mike said.

"Yeah, and maybe your parents, too," Roscoe laughed. Mike's parents were the strictest he knew. "They're going to burn your ass."

Mike smiled thinly. "You think I don't know that?" He stretched out on the deck and rolled up the pants legs on his sweatsuit. "I'm going to work on getting me a tan."

They stretched out on the deck with their hands behind their heads, not really talking much. Every once in a while they'd turn to each other and try to brag about what they'd been through, and every now and then they'd remark about how fast the water was receding. But for the most part, they were exhausted and terribly sad about losing Buckles. Suddenly Roscoe sat up. "Man, dude! Look at this. Army men!"

A small motorboat came in close to shore and two men dressed in National Guard uniforms got out and pulled it up on the beach. They started across the flattened dunes toward the boys.

Mike's grin faded. The men were unslinging their M-16s. "What in the hell, now? We're going to be shot or something?"

The tallest guardsman stopped just short of the deck. "You boys, take it easy and just come down the steps slowly."

Roscoe and Mike couldn't believe that after all they'd already been through, two rifles were pointed right at them.

Roscoe's voice was shaking. "Listen, can y'all help us? We've been on this damn island all night."

The other guardsman looked confused, but kept his gun at the ready. "We're thinking that maybe you boys might be looters."

Mike was holding his hands up in the air. "Man, you got to be kidding. We've been out here all night. We almost got killed."

Then suddenly, the long night, losing Buckles, and now having guns pointed at them, overwhelmed them. As if on cue, they both started crying.

The two guardsmen, who were no more than nineteen, looked at each other and then, slinging their gunstraps back on their shoulders, they came up on the porch. "Okay, troops," the tall one said. "It's going to be all right."

Roscoe started talking a mile a minute about everything: the surge, the house falling apart right under them, Buckles, the tornado. He told them about the snakes and the cats, even the ducks. Finally, after Roscoe calmed down and the guardsmen sat down on the porch with them, Mike told them their names.

The shorter one was lighting a cigarette. "Everybody thinks you kids are dead. They're out looking for your bodies right now."

Roscoe shuddered. The other guardsman pulled out his note-book and read them Mrs. Mary Dubose Derrick's Charleston phone number. "Do you know where this is?"

Roscoe piped up, "Yessir, it's my grandmother's! She lives down on East Bay Street. Hey, y'all didn't happen to find a yellow Labrador, did you?"

"No, I'm afraid not. We're going to try to get a call through, but we're not guaranteeing anything. It's a mess in town."

He looked them over again but this time with a mixture of curiosity and amusement. "You must have had one helluva night out here."

Roscoe, who knew he was safe and going home now, nudged Mike with his elbow. "Oh, I don't know. Actually, when you get right down to it, it was pretty cool. Right, Mike?"

Mike looked surprised. Then he caught on and, pursing his lips as if he were thinking about it, he said, "Yeah, I'd go along with that."

14 ⚡

A Legacy of Disaster

Even before Hurricane Hugo, Charleston had been the scene of more disasters than possibly any city in the country. Not only plagued with smallpox and malaria epidemics, enormous fires, and a major hurricane in 1893, but it was also hit in 1886 by the biggest earthquake ever recorded east of the Rockies; sixty people were killed and much of the city was reduced to rubble. It seems unfair (but not unlikely, then) that Hugo, the most destructive U.S. storm in this century, would not only strike South Carolina but would strike Charleston dead center. And it can certainly be predicted that, along with past natural disasters, the Civil War, and slavery, Hugo will now enter the city's mythology—a legacy that artists have been drawing on since Charleston was first settled.

Block for block in the old Historic District there is more than enough grist for the mills of writers, historians, painters, and photographers. Not only did slavery and "The War Between the States" get their start here. This is the city which, during the secession debates, stated that if South Carolina didn't secede from the Union, it would secede from South Carolina.

While this dark legacy of events and pronouncements fills the city, there is also a certain vulnerable charm there that cannot be denied. For where else but Charleston will you find basket weavers, flower ladies, shrimpers, oystermen? Where else will you hear the Gullah dialect spoken and see the Charleston danced where it began? Nowhere but in this city. DuBose Heyward, who made his living in insurance and lived in Charleston all his life, heard the street criers only a few blocks from where he lived near Cabbage Row, which is at 89–91 Church Street. Heyward changed Cabbage Row to Catfish Row, and set his famous novel *Porgy* there, later popularized in Gershwin's opera *Porgy and Bess.*

George Gershwin also heard the street criers when he came to Charleston in 1934 to work with Heyward on the stage show; he stayed on Folly Beach at 706 West Ashley Avenue. Heyward recalls taking him to a black church service. "I shall never forget the night when, at a Negro meeting on a remote sea island, George started shouting with them, and eventually to their huge delight stole the show from their champion 'shouter.' I think that he is probably the only white man in America who could have done it." Gershwin, who was so intrigued with the rhythm and cadences of the Gullah dialect, ran the Charleston "strawberry cry" through the entire musical.

On the remote Low Country island where he stayed, Gershwin experienced what may have been a minor hurricane. "The place down here looks like a battered old South Sea island. There was a storm two weeks ago which tore down a few houses along the beach and the place is so primitive they may just let them stay that way. Imagine, there's not a telephone on the whole island. The nearest phone is ten miles away."

Charleston in the thirties was brimming with other artists as well. There was photographer Alice Huger Smith, writer Julia Peterkin, and painter Elizabeth O'Neill Verner. They, along with Heyward, lived within a mile of each other in what is now referred to as the Historic District. Elizabeth O'Neill Verner writes about how small and unusual the town was even then: "Charleston has long been a city and has very few of the characteristics of a small town. In a walk around the block, you might perhaps meet five people who are nationally known and a great number more who should be." The last is pure Charleston.

Almost one hundred years before Heyward and Peterkin were writing about Charleston, William Gilmore Simms was writing novels describing his native city too. And like those artists, Simms—whose statue still stands in White Point Gardens at the Battery—was working with the materials around him: the skyline, the dialect, the slave culture, and the difference between Charleston and the rest of the country. He was also influenced by the calamities that had beset the old town: during his lifetime the smallpox and malaria epidemics raged, and fires all but burned the city to the ground.

Simms's contemporary, Edgar Allan Poe, was also struck by the rich fabric of the area. Briefly stationed at Fort Moultrie on Sullivan's Island, Poe was so taken with the area that in three of his stories, "The Oblong Box," "The Balloon Hoax," and "The Gold Bug," it is used as a setting.

Margaret Mitchell visited Charleston enough times to learn to love it and to create Rhett Butler, who may very well be the epitome of the antebellum Charleston gentleman of trade. And while Scarlett was visiting there and still longing for Ashley and her home at Tara, she wearied of Charleston social life. She couldn't stand for people to call a "house" a "hoose" and to keep reminding her of their tradition and how well placed their families were.

The color and the texture of Charleston are so compelling that few writers who live in or visit the city can resist it. Pat Conroy went to the Citadel—the state-run military college on the Ashley River—and in almost every book he writes, there in the center or in the background is Charleston. In the novels of Josephine Humphreys you will see the spires of St. Michael's and St. George and the sun setting on the copper roofs and chimney pots; and at the heart of her novels, if you listen closely, you will hear the true ring of today's Charlestonians. In her novel *The Fireman's Fair,* Humphreys deals with the psychological effect that Hurricane Hugo had on the lives of the people—an effect not only revealing but riveting.

The list of writers, painters, composers, dancers, photographers, and architects who have been influenced by Charleston and the Low Country includes, among others, Valerie Sayers, Bret Lott, Blanche Boyd, Alexandra Ripley, Sarah Gilbert, Frank O'Neill, the historian Ted Rosengarten in McClellanville, and, on up the coast at Murrell's Inlet (where his house was badly damaged by Hurricane Hugo), Mickey Spillane.

Elizabeth O'Neill Verner was right when she wrote about so much happening in "so small a place." For while it's small and at times breathtakingly beautiful, it's also crowded with incident and "firsts." It is there that indigo, rice, and cotton were first grown and exported, there that the first American theater opened, the first horse race run, and the first golf club formed. Charleston may very well be the first American city to promote tourism. In 1857 John Irving wrote, "All who come to Charleston during race week, do not find their way there merely to see the races. Many choose that time for a visit to the city. Much money is foolishly spent but whatever is spent in this way circulates freely."

Since 1977 the city has attracted visitors for another reason. Gian Carlo Menotti, after visiting the city and declaring that it was a perfect place for artists, decided that Charleston was where he wanted to bring the international cultural festival that he had been staging in Spoleto, Italy, since 1957. Menotti brought in the best in the arts from around the world: the Eliot Feld Ballet, the Westminster Choir, the Queen of Spades, a Tennessee Williams drama premiere, along with jazz, chamber music, dance, lecture, film, and street theater. Of the first U.S. Spoleto festival, *Newsweek* reported that "this bill of fare is like nothing else on the international scene, and Charleston is proud of it." Today, the festival is fifteen years old and Menotti is still in charge, and it seems to get stronger and better each year.

In the months that followed Hugo, the rumors were out that because of the incredible damage to the city and the surroundings, Spoleto would be canceled. But Menotti, a true impresario, enlisted the full support of Charlestonians, who in typical fashion were somehow strengthened by the disaster, and managed to turn the 1990 festival into one of the greatest successes yet.

―――

While the water had flooded the bottom floor of Mrs. Derrick's house on East Bay Street, most of the damage was where a lamppost had crashed onto the side porch. Unlike the four or five thousand roofs in Charleston that had been torn apart by Hugo, Mary Dubose's tin roof had held up.

The storm had stopped around 4 A.M. Shortly afterward, the police arrived with Jay and Billy wrapped up in olive drab army blankets. Mary Dubose hugged and kissed them, and as J.C. quizzed them about Roscoe and Mike, she served them each a small glass of brandy. Then, after they'd changed to some dry clothes, they all pitched in and tried to get the water and the mud out of the first floor.

It was just before dawn when J.C. realized he could no longer wait for the police. He had to do something, or he felt he would go crazy. Without telling his mother or the boys anything, he slipped outside and started walking down East Bay Street heading for the Cooper River Bridge. He was still clinging to the hope that maybe Roscoe and Mike could have left Sullivan's Island before the surge hit.

J.C. kept being stopped by the police and the National Guardsmen who were patrolling, but when he told them his story and showed them his driver's license, they let him through.

He made his way slowly and painfully through the drizzle, the trash, and the glass. The damage was unbelievable. At one point there were three trees stacked one on top of the other, and he had to climb a fence to get around them. As he worked his way through the branches and the debris he realized that he didn't know how to even comprehend this kind of disaster. Phone poles and trees were speared into the sides and roofs of houses, and entire walls had been stripped completely away. One living room, complete with lamps, a La-Z-Boy recliner, and a television set, was just sitting there, exposed to the outside, as if waiting for the owner to come home from work, turn the set on, sit down, and pop open a beer.

Glass, garbage, street signs, and billboards covered the sidewalks, the yards, and the bushes, and had blown up into the few trees that were still standing. Tin roofs and long stretches of porch screen were wrapped like ribbons around the lampposts and were flapping in the trees like so much laundry. Cars were on top of cars, boats on top of boats, and whole sides of houses and whole rooms of furniture had been scattered around as if a forty-foot Mixmaster had come through. Everywhere he turned there were magnolia and oak trees uprooted and sprawling across the streets and leaning against the houses. For a while he thought that every tree in Charleston had fallen. He saw where a flock of chickens had huddled together to drown in the grease pit of a service station. There were dead squirrels everywhere. Cutting across a backyard, he saw what looked like a patchwork quilt on a clothesline. But when he got closer he saw that it was two robins, a blackbird and a blue jay stuffed into the mesh of a steel fence.

As he worked his way through the trees, the fences, the broken glass, and the electric lines, he heard himself repeating over and over again, "Please, Lord, let my boy live. Please, Lord. Please." Then he realized he wasn't praying for Mike, and quickly changed it to, "Please, Lord, both of them. Roscoe and Mike. Please, Lord, they're only sixteen."

Finally one of the National Guardsmen who stopped J.C. realized what bad shape he was in and walked him to the police station. There they found a sergeant, and after J.C. told him the story of Roscoe and Mike, he checked a list and shook his head. "Sorry, sir, but there was no one out there that we know about."

J.C. was shouting and out of control. "Dammit! Somebody must know something!"

The guardsman who had brought him in laid his hand on his

shoulder and calmed him down. "Take it easy, Mr. Derrick, we're checking everything out. Why don't you go on home now and get some rest, and the minute we get anything I'll send somebody over."

As J.C. started to leave the station, another sergeant called out, "Derrick! Wait a minute." He turned to see a black patrolman coming down the steps leading a yellow Labrador. The sergeant grinned. "You know this dog? They just brought him in. Picked him up in the channel. We think he swam all the way over from Sullivan's Island. At least that's what his tags read."

"Buckles! Jesus, that's Buckles. He was with the kids. Come here, boy. Come on," J.C. was slapping his thighs and whistling.

Buckles jumped all over him and he wrassled his head. "Is it okay if I take him with me? I know the owners."

"Sure thing, he's all yours. I gave him two cans of food, so he shouldn't be too hungry."

Handing J.C. a piece of rope, the sergeant said, "He had this around his belly. Looks like somebody tied him to something."

J.C. fingered the end of the rope, figuring that Roscoe had cut him loose. Now he was determined more than ever that nothing was going to keep him off the island. He knew that the Ben Sawyer Bridge was out, but he also knew there were boats right across the Cooper River Bridge on the Mt. Pleasant side, and he thought he knew where he could find one.

All along Meeting Street, as he got near the Cooper River Bridge, the electrical lines were down. Many had wrapped around the trees and snapped. The power was off, but he knew they could still be hot if someone had hooked up a generator. Carefully he walked around the exposed wires and carefully he listened, trying to hear if the power was on. Most of the houses in the black neighborhoods had lost their roofs and porches, and many of the walls had been torn away, exposing bedrooms, kitchens, and bathrooms. A toilet had miraculously managed to get stuck inside a telephone booth and the strange twosome had come to rest under a chinaberry tree in a churchyard. Two teenagers stood near it, laughing.

Storefronts had lost their big windows, and the glass was all over—stuck in the scraggly hedges and in the trees and covering the street. Although it was barely daybreak, the chainsaws were already screaming away at the wet wood, trying to make a path for emergency vehicles.

J.C. knew the back streets from his boyhood, and for a while nobody bothered him or worried that he was a looter. As he walked along he kept rubbing Buckles behind the ears and saying, "That-a-boy, good dog. Good dog."

It was when they began working their way to the Cooper River Bridge that J.C. was stopped, twice—once by a guardsman who let him through, and a second time by one who had already heard about him and his lost boy. Both times he said he was on his way to find Roscoe and Mike.

After getting through the fallen trees and debris, he arrived at the Cooper River Bridge. As he expected, it was closed to everything but emergency equipment. National Guardsmen had been called in to stop the looting and were standing at parade rest with rifles and bayonets.

J.C. talked to the commanding officer of the unit, Captain Lacey, and told her that his son and his buddy were out on Sullivan's Island and he was determined to get there. The captain, a black woman wearing horn-rimmed glasses and carrying a pistol in a holster, seemed not to be listening. Then she said, "Mister Derrick, officially my hands are tied and I just can't let you go out there. But if I happen to walk over to the Port-O-Let for a few minutes, I don't think anyone is going to be breaking their neck to stop you."

J.C. thanked her and as she headed for the Port-O-Let, he and Buckles started over the mile-long bridge. About a block up, on the first span, an army jeep pulled up with Captain Lacey driving. "Hop in," she said. "I'll give you a lift."

As they rode on across the bridge, J.C. saw the aircraft carrier *Yorktown* off to the right at Patriot's Point. It seemed to have ridden the storm out with no damage, but all the land behind it, including the golf course, was completely underwater. Everywhere he looked he saw where the surge had hit, and he had to force himself not to think of how bad it really must have been for Roscoe and Mike.

When they finally crossed through the town of Mt. Pleasant and arrived at the Ben Sawyer Bridge, he saw that he wasn't the only one who wanted to get out to Sullivan's Island. There were at least two hundred residents begging and pleading with the guardsmen to take them across so they could see if their homes were lost or damaged. One couple was shouting that a hard rain was coming and they wanted to protect their property. But the police weren't listening to anyone.

Captain Lacey shook her head, "I'm sorry, Mr. Derrick, but I can't do a thing here. I figured this would happen, but I thought we'd give it a try."

J.C. shook her hand. "You did what you could. Thanks anyway."

She smiled at him and added, "If it's any help, we've all heard about the boys and everyone's out looking for them. Come on, I'll give you a ride back."

J.C. thanked her and said, "I think I just want to be alone for a while. I'll be okay, and, hey, thanks for everything."

He walked down the shoreline with Buckles, looking up and down the pier for a fishing boat, but there weren't any. Finally, and desperately, he worked his way down to the channel determined that he was going to swim across the chopping waters and then walk the rest of the way. But as he was sitting on the ground and taking his shoes off, two officers trotted over and told him to not even think about it. Their walkie-talkies were crackling with incoming information. One of the officers said, "All right," into the receiver and then gave J.C. a hand and pulled him up.

"Captain Lacey says she'll drive you back over to Charleston. We'll call you if we hear anything. You have no idea how many men are out there right now searching for those boys."

"But you don't understand," J.C. said, holding his head between his hands. Buckles wasn't moving from between his legs. "Those are my boys. My boys." Somehow, right at that moment, Mike seemed just as much his son as Roscoe.

"Yes sir, Mr. Derrick, we understand."

Captain Lacey drove J.C. and Buckles all the way back to his mother's house. He got out, thanked her, and watched her driving off. He didn't realize that as she was driving, she was talking on her walkie-talkie to all the guardsmen in her unit, and once again telling them to keep a sharp lookout for the boys.

Captain Lacey was at her post at the foot of the Cooper River Bridge when the call came through. The boys had been found and, except for some cuts and bruises, they were alive and healthy. She pushed the speaker button and said, "This is Captain Lacey. Put Mister Roscoe Derrick on a minute."

There was some crackling and then Roscoe said, "Yes, ma'am?"

Captain Lacey introduced herself and then said, "I'm taking a U-turn right now, heading to your grandmother's. Your Dad's going to be one happy man, son."

"Him and me both," Roscoe laughed.

Captain Lacey said, "Listen, I'm only a few minutes from the house. Let's just keep this line open. I want to see his face when he hears your voice."

The knock came on the door about the time J.C. had convinced himself that Roscoe was dead. He was just about to take Jay up to a quiet room and talk about it. Maybe he could prepare him. And then he had to call Beth-Ellen and tell her the news.

That's when he heard a loud knock on his mother's front door. He figured three officially dressed men would be standing behind the door, maybe carrying Roscoe's body in their arms, or worse, maybe just his shoes. Mary Dubose was pushing her way through the mud on the floor, heading for the door. "Son, I'll get it. It's probably nothing."

J.C. held her shoulder. "No, Mom, this one is mine." He opened the door slowly as he heard a woman speaking into a walkie-talkie. "Okay, that's it. That's fine."

J.C. stood in the doorway dumbfounded. Captain Lacey was speaking again. "Okay, try it again. Now, say hello to you-know-who."

Roscoe screamed. "Dad! Dad! Is that you, Dad?"

J.C. wanted to scream that it was him but all that came out was a whisper. "Yeah, Bub, it's me. It's your dad. Damn, this is terrific!"

"Dad, we're on a Coast Guard boat and it's really cool. You should see it."

"And Mike's with you? He's okay?"

"He's okay too."

J.C. wanted to hear Roscoe's voice forever but all he could think of to say was, "Well, say hello for me, okay?"

"I sure will. Dad, they want me to get off this phone now. I'll see you soon."

J.C. said, "I love you, Bub."

"Me too, Dad. I love you, too."

15 ~

Pluff Mud

In 1740, under a grant from King Charles II, William Mc-
Clellan's family settled in what was to become the town of
McClellanville, where they have been ever since and will probably remain forever. The address is 718 Pinckney Street. Until
recently there were no street numbers in this tiny fishing village forty miles north of Charleston because everyone knew
everyone else and there was no need. But in 1980, to help para-
medics to provide better service to the elderly, the old antebellum houses out under the thousand-year-old, sweeping live
oaks were numbered.

On the day before Hugo struck, William McClellan and his
sister Mary, who both now live in Columbia, evacuated their
mother, Patricia, from their house and didn't return until Sun-
day, three days later. When they did return the town had been
sealed off as a major disaster area by the National Guard; no
one was being allowed in unless he had positive proof of own-
ing a house. McClellan used his tax notice for identification
and he, his sister, and their mother were escorted into a town
they barely recognized.

Now, more than three years later, McClellan says that what
he saw that day was something so terrible and heartbreaking
that it still makes him shudder. "It was like a war had been
fought here. People were still wandering around in a daze.
There was nowhere to go. There was nothing to do. There
was absolutely no place to begin. No one asked 'what did you
lose?' or anything like that. They just assumed you'd lost
everything, and most of them had. Some of the houses were

completely gone, and pine trees and water oaks were piled everywhere. Why we didn't lose a single live oak I don't know, but we lost almost everything else. Anyhow, the trees were on top of houses, on top of cars, on top of one another. And cars and boats and pickup trucks looked like they'd been scattered around by a kid in a sandbox. It was a miracle how anyone had gotten through the night. My friend, Tommy Duke, who owns Bull Bay Seafood, said when he went out at dawn, right after the storm had gone through, he expected to see bodies floating everywhere."

William McClellan brought along a camera on the day he returned. "I stood in one spot and took four shots, one in each direction. One was of two big, sixty-foot shrimp boats piled on top of each other. One was of three red pickups that had been thrown out into the water. One was a boat on top of a house, and one was a boat on top of a house that had been completely flattened by the surge. And imagine, that was all from one spot. I still have trouble looking at the shots. It was awful."

McClellanville and Jeremy Creek are protected from the ocean by the Cape Romain salt marsh. While the creek meanders over eight miles to the ocean through the marsh and the Intracoastal Waterway, as the crow flies it is only three miles. Carolina Seafood and Bull Bay Seafood operate out of the harbor, and for years it was considered one of the snuggest and safest harbors on the coast. The operative word is "was," because on September 21 at 11:38 P.M., when Hugo struck at high tide, that ten-foot wall of water funneled up Jeremy Creek getting higher and stronger until, when it hit and devastated the tiny village, it was an unbelievable twenty-three feet.

McClellanville, which may very well have been one of the most charming and picturesque fishing villages on the coast, is probably best known for its Bull Bay oysters and its shrimp, but it was also famous for its annual blessing of the fleet ceremony sponsored by the Episcopal church every spring. Eight months after the surge had virtually wiped out the town, William McClellan and his friends were determined that, despite the destruction, the town would once again have the blessing. "You see, we wanted desperately for things to get back to normal. Even though we knew they never would."

The blessing did take place on May 10, 1990, but of the forty-odd boats that would normally be there, only twenty were back in order. The priest blessed the fleet and the crowd and said a prayer of thanksgiving, but as he did so, almost everyone standing there was reliving the terrible Thursday night and Friday morning when Hugo swept through, leaving their world so changed it would never ever be the same.

Debbie Thomas, who lives in town, said, "I don't know if I can ever listen to the wind again and not get scared."

And Mary Linen: "When I lay down on the pillow, the tears just flow. I have nightmares. Like I'm fighting for my life again. But I still say we are blessed. Everyone wants to come back. If we didn't, we'd pass by all this."

McClellan explained that the blessing had a reverse effect on many people and almost backfired. "Right after the storm people thought that with time they could salvage some things. But the more time that went by, the more they realized how much else they had lost. I'll give you one example. See, we had no idea that *all* of the insulation in the house was contaminated with salt water and pluff mud [a mix of silt and salt and marsh]. It had to be removed or the house would simply rot. And to remove it you had to either take the Sheetrock off from inside, or the wall siding from the outside. In either case, you had to literally strip the house down to the studs.

"I didn't know a lot about pluff mud before, but I sure as hell know a lot about it now. First of all, once it's in your house, it's almost impossible to get rid of. We had six inches and it must have stayed there for months before we got it all out. It gets into everything, and with the combination of saltwater it ruins everything.

"But back to the blessing. People knew they'd lost their mattresses and rugs and things like that, but it took months for them to realize how much else was ruined. Take furniture: almost every piece of furniture that had been manufactured in the last forty years was ruined. I didn't believe it at first, but here's what happened: anything glued or laminated was lost. It just broke down. The glue melted and the lamination just came apart. Screws or nails or staples rusted and dropped out.

"I'm talking about whole living rooms, whole dining rooms, whole bedroom suites—everything. I'm talking about pictures on the walls, mirrors, mantelpieces, everything. You name it and it was ruined. The only, and I mean the *only,* furniture my mother saved was some old maple chairs and a table that had been built around 1900 when they were still using wooden pegs to hold them together. Everything else put together with screws or nails or glue had to be thrown away. Oh, we did manage to save some glass and china, but we were warned that if the mud got in the pots and pans, which it did, we were to throw them away because they were containing poisons which would come out when they were heated."

One of the saddest sights for William McClellan was the endless rows of mattresses that lined the streets. "You'd see them everywhere and they stayed out there for months, and you can imagine how hard it was to drag a soaking mattress out of a house. And Lord, almost none of the new ones have handles."

During the storm surge the water level in the McClellan living room was over four feet. Outside it was over ten, but the house was strong and tight and didn't leak as much as many of the others in town. But, like every house, theirs was swamped with pluff mud. "While we were cleaning it out," McClellan recalled, "our shoes would get clogged up and so heavy we could barely move. As a matter of fact, we'd have to wipe them off before we went outside so we could walk."

Many of the McClellanville homes were insured for wind

damage. Unfortunately, while wind damage covers a tree punching a hole in a roof and causing leakage, it does not include storm surge damage. The logic of this is curious but sufficient to satisfy the insurance companies: if the wind throws a tree onto your house it's one thing, but if it hurls twenty-three feet of water into your house it's quite another. Since the wind that pushed the tree is the same wind that pushed the surge, this seems to place the insurance companies in the dubious position of blaming the surge on some mysterious force other than the 168-mph spiral of wind and cloud that was Hugo. But then that's what lawyers get paid for. This little semantic shuffle saved insurance companies millions of dollars in McClellanville, where most of the damage was due to the terrible surge, and it has left the majority of the people, who had only wind damage insurance, with almost nothing.

"No one wants to tie up their lives suing an insurance company to get this wind damage wrinkle ironed out," McClellan said. "But I sure wish someone would. That little clause has ruined more lives than you can imagine. You see, people didn't just lose some things, they lost everything, and most of it was due to the surge."

McClellan said that while there was some looting, it was minor. "There's always going to be some during something like this. But I'd say there was very little here. Everyone had lost almost everything and we were all in this thing together. Hell, there was nothing left to loot."

The McClellan family is now in the process of rebuilding the old house at 718 Pinckney and, despite the difficulties and the expenses, some of the good memories of the aftermath of the storm are now beginning to push away the bad. "People came from everywhere to help us," McClellan recalled. "New Jersey even adopted us. Ken Hyatt is this automobile dealer from Batesburg, you see him on TV all the time. He does his own ads. Well, he pulled in here with his RV and set up a big grill and he got in there behind it and all he did for three or four days was fry and make hamburgers and cheeseburgers. Everybody was like that. I've never seen such hard workers and such outright generosity. You'd see volunteers chasing down people and forcing money on them. I mean a hundred dollars, two hundred dollars. And these were total strangers and it was happening all over the place. God, I think we all went a little crazy there for a while trying to help one another. I know I did. Hell, I was hugging people I barely knew."

Around 3 A.M., as the winds began to abate and the water began to recede, Jennings Austin, Edward Smith, and Charles DuTart eased back through the top of the classroom window and lowered themselves back into the five feet of water in the school. Jennings led the way as they waded and swam through the classroom and out into the long hall that led to the cafeteria. He was petrified, afraid of what he knew he was about to see, and was trying to steel himself for it. Part of him wanted to delay it, but a much bigger part kept insisting that someone might still be alive. Someone might need him.

It had been dark outside and it was dark in the classroom, but the auxiliary lights in the hallway were still on and they could see all the way to the end. Jennings groaned when he realized that all he was seeing in the eerie light was the dark water. There was nothing else. There was no sound, no movement, and he was now certain that every one of the kids, teenagers, and adults had all perished, and perished horribly.

He had gone only a few more yards when he saw the beam of a flashlight. Then he heard a voice. He knew that voice from the baseball field: it was Coach Melvin Powell. Jennings shouted out. "Coach! Is that you, Coach?"

"Yeah, Jennings, where in the hell you been?"

Jennings rushed, waded, and swam down the hall as fast as he could. If Powell was alive, maybe there were others. Then he saw

Powell smile. "We've been looking all over for you. Everybody thought y'all got killed."

Jennings relaxed for the first time in hours, and kept sloshing toward him. "I can't believe it. I swear to God, I can't believe it."

They were finally close enough to hug each other and Jennings said, "I thought you all were the dead ones."

Powell laughed, "Well, I guess we just got lucky. It was close there for a while."

Jennings made his way into the cafeteria and saw what had happened. Everyone was still up on the stage. Some were standing in water up to their waists and armpits, while others were standing on the tables with the water only up to their knees. The water was receding; at the high water mark it had reached almost seven feet, now it was less than three. Everyone was talking, but many were whispering. They were still scared.

For a while, it drizzled, then a heavy rain started and lasted until it was almost light. But then, as soon as the day dawned, the rain stopped and the sun came up. The clouds rolled back, revealing a beautiful, clear blue sky. The people began pouring out of the school into the three feet of water that stretched all the way across the parking lot. The small kids were too short for the water and the women held them on their hips; the men slung them up on their shoulders. The old folks gathered in the sunshine near the door, where the water was shallower.

After a while everyone was outside standing in the sunshine and the water. From a distance it looked like a giant baptismal pool as families and friends were wading back and forth and coming together. They were hugging one another and laughing, hugging one another and crying, and just hugging one another and looking for somebody else to hug. There had never been so much joy and happiness, so much profound relief. There was no talk of houses, or furniture, or boats being lost. That would come soon enough. But for the moment, no one cared what they had lost, or what they were about to lose. All they were concerned about was the simple, solid fact that they and their families and their friends were alive. It was a miracle. The only casualty was the Reverend Steven A. Sheppard, who had suffered a heart attack and would later die in the hospital. Everyone else was present and accounted for; Sharon Brown's baby would arrive a few days late, but she would be as healthy as her mother.

Horace was holding onto Wanda and Tonya's legs. He had one girl on each shoulder. And Joe was holding Molly by her front feet to keep her nose out of the water. Every time Horace thought about how brave his daughters had been he almost wept. He couldn't wait to see Olly May and have her see them. She was probably scared out of her wits not knowing what had happened. God knows what they had been broadcasting on the television and radio. Someone had already told Horace that his house was gone, but he still didn't know about his boat. He knew he could build the house back. And if he lost his boat, well, he could rebuild that, too, or get another one. But there was one casualty he was going to have to face. Rambo, his dog, the dog Olly May had given him for a birthday present five years ago, was gone. Without making a sound, the dog had gone under right below where the twins had spent the night up in the ceiling crawlspace. Horace knew he was going to have to tell them sometime soon, but right now, with all the celebrating going on, was not the time. Joe shoved a pint of whiskey into his hand. Shifting sideways to lean against the building and balance the girls better, Horace took a long, long-deserved drink. Then he grinned at Joe and had another.

One group of ladies, with their dresses ballooning out around them, began singing "Rock of Ages." Their voices rose in the still air and rolled out across the strange water they were standing in. As the singing swelled and could be heard all the way across the lot and out into the trees, other voices joined in and the old song came echoing back. It came back to them from the cars and the pickup trucks and the debris of mobile homes and chifforobes stacked up against the school wall. And it echoed back from the twisted, broken houses and trailers and shrimp boats of McClellanville and the thousand trees lying around them. More and more voices joined in and the singers were now raising their faces to the bluest sky they had ever seen, and if ever a man was relieved to be standing in three feet of water and singing his heart out on September the twenty-second, 1989, it was the school principal, Mr. Jennings Austin.

Down on the dock, half a mile away, there was another celebration going on. The crew members of the good ship *Mermaid,* Capt. Stan Salter's boat, were sitting on the deck drinking their first beer and toasting the longest six hours they had ever known. The beer was hot because the refrigeration had been out since the storm struck, but it was still the best beer any of the men had ever tasted. They toasted Hugo. They toasted the *Mermaid.* And they toasted Stan Salter. But they saved the best toast for last. They toasted the simple fact that they were alive.

Around him and as far as Salter could see, nothing had escaped the wrath of the storm. Houses and boats and stores were either badly damaged or completely destroyed. Of the twenty-eight boats that had been tied to the dock, only his and two others had survived. He could now make out what he thought was Joe's boat, thrown up into the woods. It was in terrible shape. The whole front end was stove in, and he knew there was almost no chance of salvaging it.

Salter would be the first to admit that he had been foolish not going to Jacksonville earlier, but now he was glad he'd ridden Hugo out and, as he drank his beer, he swore to himself that wild horses and a million dollars wouldn't make him do it again.

He finished his beer and, after popping open a second and turning up the radio they had been listening to all night long, he began laughing. The *Mermaid* had been able to get only one station, and that station had recorded a message at 9:15 Thursday night that had played over and over and over again. It was still playing. "Miami Hurricane Center is now reporting that Hurricane Hugo will not be hitting the South Carolina coast. . . . Miami Hurricane Center is now reporting that Hurricane Hugo will not be hitting the South Carolina coast. . . . Miami Hurricane Center. . . ."

16

The Wind Returneth

For the five years before Hugo hit South Carolina, the golf courses at Kiawah and Wild Dunes, located only twenty-odd miles from downtown Charleston, had been rated by the major golf magazines among the top ten golf resorts in the United States and among the top twenty in the world. During Hugo, Kiawah, which is an island south and to the east of Charleston, sustained wind damage to its trees and a loss of power from the mainland, but within four weeks all three of its golf courses were cleaned up, back in shape, and open to the public. Not only was the famous resort open, but golf architect Pete Dye was busy laying out the Ocean Course, the site of the prestigious 1991 Ryder Cup matches between the United States and Europe.

On the way to Kiawah, the golfer passes by the Angel Oak, a sprawling and absolutely awesome live oak that is probably more than two thousand years old. The morning after Hugo a few of the faithful, scared that the old oak had been damaged, rushed out U.S. 17, turned left at Bohicket Road, and turned off at the dirt road to see the tree. The group could not believe their eyes—at a time when live oaks in the area sustained tremendous damage, their prayers had been answered. The tree was intact.

Wild Dunes, a resort to the north of Charleston on the Isle of Palms, not only caught the full 150-mph brunt of the storm, but was swamped by a twenty-foot tidal surge that was nothing short of catastrophic. Both its golf courses, the Links and the Harbor, were inundated with five to six feet of saltwater;

the wind damage to trees was incredible—the estimate is that more than a thousand fell or were irreparably damaged. In addition, at least thirty boats from the marina and ten or twelve houses from the Wild Dunes village were washed out onto the fairways. The first reports claimed that the famous seventeenth and eighteenth holes on the Links Course had washed away—and that neither course would ever recover. The reports were wrong. Within weeks there was a mammoth reconstruction program under way to save the holes and the courses, and in a few months both were in playable shape and booked solid.

Across the bay on U.S. 17, north of Mt. Pleasant, the Charleston National Course, a beautiful Rees Jones layout built on a bluff overlooking the waterways and the marshes, was almost destroyed. Most of its trees were uprooted by the wind, and new channels cut through the fairways. But the management hired the architect to come back and rebuild the layout. Today, three years later, the course is back in shape and may very well be better than ever.

Yeaman's Hall, one of the most exclusive clubs in the country (in 1925 when it opened, the Yale golf team came down from New Haven in a private car for the ceremonies), sustained heavy tree losses, but they too are back in business. And Charleston Country Club, on record as being the first golf club in America, dating back to 1786, also suffered major tree damage and roof damage to the old club house. Hilton Head, to the north, the sea island with the most golf courses and the biggest reputation, was barely touched.

Three years after Hugo all of the golf courses that had been hit and damaged around Charleston and on up the coast to Myrtle Beach were back in shape and back in business. As with Charleston itself, which soon cleared away the trees and fallen branches and put on a cheerful outward face for the tourists and visitors, the resorts were welcoming visitors from across the United States to neatly tended grounds, painstakingly landscaped to erase all traces of storm damage. But if you know where to look, and know what was there before, you can still see evidence of Hugo's fury. And in the small towns and rural communities where the storm's force was greatest and the spotlight of publicity did not reach, even someone unfamiliar with what was there before can see the storm's legacy. More than three years later, places like McClellanville, Summerville, Florence, Camden, and a dozen others were still cleaning up and still rebuilding.

Six weeks after Hugo, the Salvation Army and the American Red Cross sponsored a benefit concert for the relief of storm victims at the Carolina Coliseum in Columbia, featuring Barry Manilow. The response from South Carolinians was overwhelming, and relief continued to pour in from throughout the United States, despite the near-simultaneous disaster of a major earthquake in the Bay Area of California. Maj. Ken Bush, who headed up the Salvation Army in South Carolina, seemed very pleased as he sat back with his hands behind his head in his Columbia office. "Every disaster I've worked has had this wonderful compassionate feeling about it. But South Carolinians surpassed anything I've ever seen—it was like it was one big family—blacks and whites together—I've never seen anything quite like it."

He went on to say that corporate response to calls for aid was swift and substantial. "It looked like they just opened their warehouses and gave us everything we could possibly use. I mean everything. Not one company refused us or cut back on what they had promised. They also got everything they promised us here to Columbia on time. It was a wonderful thing to see."

Among those companies sending supplies were Procter and Gamble (Pampers and Jif peanut butter), Colgate (toothbrushes, toothpaste, soaps), Gillette (deodorant and shaving supplies), Ralston Purina (dog food), Anheuser-Busch (cans of water delivered in Budweiser cans), Frito-Lay (Corn Chips and Corn Curls), Curtis Candy (Baby Ruth bars), Publix Food Stores of Florida (six trailer-loads of oranges), Planters Peanuts (peanuts and candy), and the Billy Graham Association (twenty trailers of food and clothing).

These shipments arrived in Columbia in forty-eight-foot tractor trailers at a rate of ten per day for three solid weeks. Major Bush said that trying to unload and repack the big trucks and put the material in smaller trucks and distribute them to the proper places was an enormous logistical job. The first thing he did was to send out a call for help from the trucking industries. "It was amazing. Every state in the nation sent trucks. Every one of them. And without them we couldn't have done it."

Major Bush said sometimes the problem was having too many supplies in one spot. "When TV showed how hard McClellanville had been hit, Toms River, New Jersey, stepped in and said they were adopting the town. A couple of days later thirteen forty-eight-foot trailers of material arrived. All of a sudden we had so many trucks and rigs and supplies in that tiny town that we couldn't move."

During the two weeks after Hugo, the Salvation Army distributed the following items in South and North Carolina:

Sandwiches and meals	557,983
Drinks and coffee	432,129
Food bags	338,400
Baby needs	122,570
Clothing	809,045
Bags of ice	682,850

Major Bush was also happy to report that one of the best things to come out of the storm and the aftermath was the realization of the need for Salvation Army shelters in Kingstree, St. Andrews, and Georgetown, South Carolina. Since Hugo, these shelters have been put into place and are now working and operating to feed and clothe the homeless.

Right after the storm, the only restaurant with power in Columbia was the old Capitol on Main Street, which stayed open around the clock. The owner, John Forrester, said he must have served five thousand orders of grits and eggs and sausage and ten thousand cheeseburgers to the evacuees up from Charleston and the Low Country. And some of his faithful customers reported that he must have said, "this one's on the house," to half of Clarendon County. In the aftermath there had been talk of canceling the USC-Clemson game, but reason prevailed and three weeks later Clemson cakewalked up and down the field to the tune of 45 to 0. By this time Piggly Wiggly, Kroger, and Winn-Dixie had restocked their shelves and the price of 87 octane unleaded at the self-serve pump was holding at $1.10 a gallon. The evacuees finally went home and, except for tree and car damage, all was very soon back to something approaching normal in the Capitol city.

In Charleston the downed electric poles were repositioned and restrung with new lines. Transformer fuses and transformers were replaced and power was on for some within four days. For others it took weeks. One utility official said, "It was not a question of repairing the distribution system; it was a matter of rebuilding in days a system that had taken us eighty years to create." The telephone system, largely underground, was out only a few hours.

Along with rebuilding the energy infrastructure, Charleston was faced with a major problem of getting roofs and sides of houses and whole trees out of the streets. But there were other problems. On Folly Beach, Diane and Glenn Hughes found a six-foot-long porpoise in a front room of a beachfront house. They loaded it onto a fallen door, carried it down to the water, eased it into the shallows, then held it in their arms and talked to it until it got strong enough to swim. Diane Hughes said, "After about half an hour it just swam out of my arms. It never looked back." And Thelma Moore of Macedonia, South Carolina, whose daughter's trailer lost its roof, also reported,

"My son raises roosters to sell, you know, them fighting roosters. He staked them all down so they wouldn't get blowed away, and mostly they didn't. But they ain't got a feather left on them."

Back in Charleston the insurance adjusters were coming to town like gunslingers clinging to what appeared to be two sets of instructions and two only: wind damage claims were estimated at the minimum, because they were covered; flood damage was estimated at the maximum, because it was not. They were nicknamed "bounty hunters," and one of the half-joking, half-serious rumors was that they were working on commission. On Broad and Meeting streets tree limbs and broken glass were swept away, and lawyers, who seem to thrive on disaster, were having a field day taking on the adjusters. Meanwhile, out on southbound Interstate 26 and U.S. 17 heading into town, men from Georgia, Alabama, and Mississippi, looking more like hippie hitchhikers than skilled workers ready to go to work, were standing by their pickups holding signs: "Roof Man," "Tree Man," "Carpenter," "Plumber," "Stump Grinder."

Network and cable television shot the Hugo disaster as if it were an Arnold Schwarzenegger film—all action and wind and surge damage—no story. The endless footage of the Ben Sawyer Bridge cocked up in the air was nothing when compared to the drama that had gone on, and was going on, in the small towns Hugo boiled through. What television missed, and has continued to miss, were the stories behind the losses and the hidden damage. So while South Carolina has put on a brave outer face to let the tourists know that the hotels and golf courses are open and the beaches clear, under the surface are deeper scars and darker problems that are as real as the bills in the morning mail.

Major Bush, who knows the problems only too well, said the Salvation Army's biggest job would be to help people who were fighting to get out of drug and alcohol dependency cope with the additional stress of Hugo. "If these people aren't helped and helped soon they'll just drop back into their old ways. All a lot of them need is an excuse to keep on drinking and using drugs and Hugo has sure given them that. Our job is to get to them and counsel them and get them through this next period. Frankly, this is going to be much harder than serving meals and building houses."

One of the world's oldest truths is that most people are wonderful during disasters. They know that but for the grace of God it could be them, and almost immediately they drop their guard and identify with the victims. While they watch their television and see a Wild Dunes couple staring at the pilings where their beach house once stood, or read in the paper about a poor Camden man and his wife finding the trailer pad and broken hurricane straps where their mobile home had once been anchored, they, for the moment, almost become the victims themselves. True, the moment rarely lasts, but once in a while the spark ignites something bigger and people do things they never dreamed possible. The heroes and heroines of Hugo were poor people, rich people, people who had lost everything, and people who had lost nothing. Some were neighbors from down the road and some were strangers who brought their own food and slept in their own cars and stayed and helped do the hard dirty work of digging out and getting everything back to normal. What made them come can be as complicated as a Jungian analysis or as simple as the Golden Rule, but the unassailable fact is they came and they stayed until the work was finished.

Kathy Gilbert, the Hugo Relief State Chairman of the South Carolina Jaycees, tells how seventeen Jaycees drove six Ryder trucks filled with supplies all the way across the country from the state of Washington in eight days. When they arrived they insisted on unloading the trucks themselves, then took plane flights back home that same day. And she tells how the Georgia Jaycees sent in over $1.5 million worth of supplies on one trip and how, on Christmas Day, wearing Santa Claus suits, they brought an eighteen-wheeler full of toys.

A hand-printed sign at the crossroads in McClellanville reads "God Bless the Volunteers." It has been there for more than two years now, and it probably says everything the people of McClellanville wanted to say and everything the volunteers wanted to hear. Most of the tiny village has recovered and been cleaned up by now. The leaves on the live oaks are green again, and the grass and flowers that were killed by the salt water and pluff mud are growing back. Pelicans, herons, and egrets are back in attendance, and people are feeding the squirrels pecans and peanuts to tide them over until the acorns ripen. Inside Lincoln High School, the only trace of the storm is a bronze plaque in the cafeteria showing that the water level on September 22, 1989, when Hugo's tidal surge washed over everything, was six feet, eight inches. The rest of the building looks brand new.

What we have learned and profited from in the aftermath of Hugo, it turns out, has been pitifully little. We learned how to rebuild the infrastructure fast, and we learned a new way to protect the endangered red-cockaded woodpecker, using artificial nests. And that may very well be it. The bigger problems are still with us—and are getting bigger. The timber industry may very well succeed in replanting the devastated Francis Marion National Forest with mostly loblolly pines; beach developers will keep the pressure on; and at the moment there is talk in Washington of redefining wetlands so many new shore areas can be developed.

But the pelicans are back. Along with the pelicans, the shrimp and fish have come back to the area and once again the fleet is bringing its catch in to the fish houses on Jeremy Creek in McClellanville. It will be a slower recovery there, down around the dock. Five of the boats, the *Mary Anne,* the *Edisto,* the *Wasp,* the *Moonrise,* and the *Lucky Lady* are beyond repair and still lying on their sides rotting and rusting away, waiting for the bulldozer. Two others, the *Charlestonian* and the *Sun Maid,* which were flung far back into the swamp, are slowly sinking and being overgrown with moss and kudzu and will probably stay there forever.

For many of the people the shock and the loss from Hugo have been too great and the scars too deep to ever heal. Every time the clouds change color or the wind picks up, memories of the terrible night of the storm come back stronger than ever. On August 18, 1991, a month shy of the second anniversary of Hugo, Hurricane Bob threatened the coast. That hurricane didn't even come close. While there was no danger, and no evacuation was declared, many panicked and fled inland anyway. Some people still have trouble sleeping, some keep their radios on the weather station all night long, and some can't stop watching the sky and the waves and listening for the wind. And some, like a certain very thin and very old lady, wearing a wide-brimmed straw hat and sitting under a big green-and-white golf umbrella, fishing for perch and reading her Bible at the end of a dock in McClellanville, are convinced the worst is yet to come. When people stop to see the fish in her bucket she takes their arm with one hand, and turning pages with the other until she finds her place, she makes them listen to Ecclesiastes, chapter one, verse six:

The wind goeth toward the south, and turneth about unto the north; it whirleth about continually, and the wind returneth again according to His circuits.